'Margaret has proved to be th[...] broadcaster I have ever wit[...] brought comfort and happine[...]

Ian Walker, General Manager, Radio 2SM Sydney

'Your radio chat show on 2SM is very uplifting and gives a lot of comfort to those whose loved ones have left them.'

Bill, Sydney

'When God put angels on earth he sent Margaret Dent. Her gift to us is her knowledge of the spirit world. This book is a must!'

Jennifer Green, G'Day Hollywood Productions (Aust)

'When I first heard Margaret Dent doing survival evidence with callers to her radio show I couldn't believe that she wasn't being fed information. So, one night, I went to watch her work. She wasn't. Now that I have the honour to actually work with her she never ceases to amaze me. She's being fed information all right. But it's not from this world!'

Ian McCrae, Radio 2SM Sydney

'Out of all the guests I've had on air I've never received such a huge response from anyone. Margaret is great! I still can't believe it until I hear my callers talk with her. She's a great person with a great heart and a truly unbelievable gift . . . the accuracy is amazing.'

Pete McMurry, WXR 104.9FM Rockford, Illinois

'Margaret is great! She made a believer out of me. She's amazing.'

Greg Bair, Madison, Wisconsin

'People want to believe and their faith is warranted, judging by our callers' moving conversations with Margaret. Her riveting discourse coupled with her gentle disposition provide a believable, comforting experience for both caller and listener.'

Kathryn Lake, Radio Talk Show Host, Madison,
Wisconsin

'Margaret has an incredible gift. She is truly amazing. If you hear her once, you'll believe too!'

Donna, Las Vegas

'Thank you, Margaret, for giving me the belief that there is life after this one.'

Lorna, Las Vegas

LOVE NEVER DIES

Extraordinary accounts
of survival beyond death

MARGARET DENT

Bantam Books
Sydney • Auckland • Toronto • London • New York

LOVE NEVER DIES
A BANTAM BOOK

First published in Australia and New Zealand in 1999 by Bantam

National Library of Australia.
Cataloguing-in-Publication entry

Dent, Margaret, 1946– .
   Love never dies : extraordinary accounts of survival beyond death.

   ISBN 0 7338 0131 5.

   1. Dent, Margaret, 1946– . 2. Future life. 3. Psychic
   ability. 4. Psychics – Biography. I. Title.

133.9013

Bantam books are published by

Transworld Publishers
a division of Random House Australia Pty Ltd
20 Alfred Street, Milsons Point, NSW 2061

Random House New Zealand Limited
18 Poland Road, Glenfield, Auckland

Transworld Publishers (UK) Limited
61-63 Uxbridge Road, Ealing, London W5 5SA

Random House Inc
1540 Broadway, New York, New York 10036

Cover photograph by Louise Lister
Typeset in 11/12.5 pt Bembo by Midland Typesetters, Maryborough, Victoria
Printed by Griffin Press, Netley, South Australia

10 9 8 7 6 5 4 3 2 1

Dedicated to Robert John Dent – 'Bob'

Without your never-ending support, love, faith and confidence in me and my gifts there would not have been any church work leading me to teach.

Your strength is the rock I built my reputation as a professional medium on; without it I would have walked away in the first year.

With you by my side I took my first hesitant steps on radio, leading to television and public appearances. I would not have written my first book and there would not have been enough experiences to write others. The endless cups of coffee and meals as I'm writing make extra work for you; not once in 30 years have you ever complained!

You insist on standing in the background behind the scenes, where only a few people know you are there. God knows, and so do I.

Thank you, Coral, for being you. The world would be a happier place if more people were like you.

Thank you, Pauline, for always being there.

My family and friends in the spirit world. This world misses your physical presence but you keep teaching me that love never dies:

Nanna Liz, Michael, Bo-Bo, Mum, Dad, Nanna Stone, Uncle Mick, John, Ken, Ma, Frank.

Billy, Alice, Clarrie, Gladdy, Dan, Garry, Michael, Paul, Danny, Maureen, Elizabeth, Grace, Eileen.

CONTENTS

ACKNOWLEDGMENTS

WITHOUT THE LOVING SUPPORT of my teachers and guides in the spirit world this book would not be possible. I have made many friends in the spirit world while giving evidence of their survival to loved ones on earth. God bless you.

To the readers of *Conversations with the Dead*, thank you for your letters, inspiring and encouraging me to write *Love Never Dies*.

Thank you, universe, for providing that invisible thread that unites humankind in love and friendship, working its magic when Pamela Willmont introduced me to Maggie Hamilton, making the publishing of this book possible. Maggie, you share your loving light with so many people, it's a privilege to call you a friend.

Suzy, Margaret and John Yates, you shared your beautiful house overlooking the ocean with its peace and tranquillity, so necessary for Christine Segal, Julie Oliver and myself to chronicle the hundreds of cassette tapes from my radio programs. The love, patience and encouragement given to me by Julie and Christine are amongst my most treasured memories.

Desney Shoemark for the love and caring you gave to me while editing this book.

Compassion is a rare facet of human nature. For most of us it has to be nurtured through a generous and loving application of words, deeds and action in dealing with others in our daily lives. I have three friends whose compassion is their nature: Maureen Kalucy, Helen Casey and my husband Bob.

My son John gives me healing and laughter with his solid commonsense and crazy sense of humour. Biologically he is my only child but all his life he has stepped back because of the never-ending flow of people he has had to share me with. The many lifetimes we have shared give us that special bond that cannot translate into words.

PREFACE

PEOPLE ARE LOOKING FOR ANSWERS. They want to believe that there is life after death. For over thirty years now, I have taught people to develop their psychic and healing abilities. In our recently formed Spiritual Enlightenment Center based in Las Vegas, Nevada, classes and lectures based on those in Australia are being taught and developed.

In this book, I explain how my psychic ability works and how I learned to work with it. I also pass on information from my teachers in the spirit world, information you can use to develop your own psychic abilities in a sensible, harmonious way.

I am not an expert on religious matters. I am, however, experienced in what happens to people when they die. My aim is to take the fear out of this subject and to light the way for people from all walks of life. As you read on, you will realise that you can develop your own psychic abilities; that working with psychic abilities is not a game; that everyday life is the classroom, and commonsense the best teacher. What I can do, you can do – and I'm happy to share the way with you.

The stories in this book are true. They are about normal people reaching out for proof of life after death, people seeking solutions to difficult questions, people in need of healing or comfort.

I believe psychic ability provides us with the keys to unlock doors that open the way to spiritual awareness and knowledge. This enables us to progress safely beyond the psychic stage and to gain fuller realisation of our relationship with the Creator and the universe. We learn that we are spiritual beings given earthly bodies, which allow us to experience the joys and sorrows of life through our journey on the earth. We begin to understand that any path we take in our search for God leads us to the light. We start to understand that judging our fellow human beings – because they are slow to learn, or afraid to think for themselves, or unwilling to open their minds to the true spiritual aspects of life, or condemning of those who do – is the same as judging ourselves. When I need to remind myself of this lesson, this saying helps: 'There but for the grace of God go I – for it probably was I'.

People who leave the spiritual doors closed and play with the psychic keys will come to the realisation it can be dangerous and misleading, bringing them unhappiness and despair in their daily lives, continually disrupting their relationships with other people. It can cause problems with physical, emotional and mental health until one day the full realisation hits: this is not a game, and the psychic keys are not toys.

There are many of you with open minds who will immediately be able to prosper and progress as you read on – reinforcing what you already know, developing new insights into concepts you were not sure of and, hopefully, finding answers to questions about our spiritual journey through life and death.

୧୬୭

Don't be afraid to ask, 'What is my real self?'

Your strengths, your truths can be found by opening your mind to what so many people are saying. I am only one of millions who have had the same kinds of experiences.

I hope this book will help you to understand that there are people in both worlds who can help you in your search. If I can help you to overcome your fear of death, nothing life presents you with will ever make you fearful again.

Margaret Dent
Sydney, 1999

INTRODUCTION

I HAD ALWAYS BEEN DEVOTED to my younger brother, Michael, and we remained close even after both of us married.

Michael's son Christopher was two-and-a-half years old, our John was five, and Michael's wife Ann was expecting another child when Michael got news that he was to start work with the Waterside Workers Federation. At last, he would have the job he had been wanting for years. Michael had a very friendly personality and people liked him. He had many friends, the closest going back to his school days, and we had all known each other for many years.

So when he started his new job, it was as if he were in a play where all the actors were new and different, taking the place of the ones we had seen before. I didn't know his workmates or his routine any more, or where he could be located during the day. Ann and I were used to knowing what time he started work and when he would be home, but all this changed. He had a pocket-book of numbers we would have to ring. If it was raining his schedule changed, and he seldom worked in the same place twice running.

❧

I now think of the following series of events as my own 'Garden of Gethsemane' experience – remember, the place where Jesus went into a deep sleep and the soldiers came and arrested him. It was the day before Ann gave birth to their second child. I had to leave work early and go home to bed. I wasn't sick, but I couldn't stay awake. It was as though I had been drugged. When my husband, Bob, came home he cooked dinner but I was so groggy I couldn't lift my head from the pillow. All I wanted was to sleep.

When Michael phoned to say the baby had been born, Bob told him I was sick in bed. Michael called in the next day, but they decided not to disturb me, and just let me sleep on. Mum rang and I was still out to it. By the fourth day, Bob said he would have to call the doctor.

I had not congratulated Michael, and hadn't visited Ann or seen the new baby. Yet I didn't feel guilt – or any emotion for that matter. All I wanted was sleep. But I stirred myself enough to tell Bob I would go to the hospital to visit Ann and the baby that night, and asked him to tell Michael we would have a celebratory drink afterwards. This satisfied Bob that I was getting better, and he left it at that. That night he worked late and assumed I was at the hospital, but in fact I was still asleep with no concept of time or anything else.

Andrew, a friend of Michael's, offered to drive him to the hospital that same night to meet me. Since I wasn't there, Michael phoned me – but I didn't hear the phone. When visiting hours were over, Andrew suggested a few drinks because Michael hadn't yet celebrated the birth of his son. Both Michael and Ann were concerned about me and uneasy without knowing why. They just knew that no matter how sick I felt, it wouldn't have stopped me from being there.

Later, Bob came home and found me still asleep. When he woke me, however, I could sit up and my head was clear. I couldn't believe I had slept through another day and had missed Ann and Michael. I was able to get out of bed and eat something. Whatever had been wrong with me for the last few days was over. We sat in the lounge room and talked a while, but it was late and Bob was tired, so we went to bed. When the doorbell rang, Bob got up and answered it.

'It's Michael,' he said.

I went into the lounge room, and was introduced to Andrew. They had both had a lot to drink, and Andrew was definitely too drunk to be driving. If he had been one of Michael's old friends who really knew me, it might have had a different effect when I said, 'Why don't you stay the night?'

As it was, Andrew said there was nothing wrong with him and he was more than capable of driving. I didn't argue. I commented on a jumper Michael was wearing, one I hadn't seen before. His birthday was two weeks away and Mum had given it to him early so he could wear it that night when he went out. I told him how sorry I was about not seeing the baby, but he said not to worry – there would be other days. He said he had been worried about me, and had come to make sure I was all right.

I tried a different approach with Andrew, but that didn't work either. I thought he was being very foolish and decided to treat him as if he wasn't in the room. So I turned to Michael and said, 'You stay here then.'

'No,' Michael said, 'I have to work tomorrow.'

'Then I'll drive you home, because he's too drunk to drive.'

'Margaret,' he said, 'I've been out with him all night. He drove me to the hospital and brought me here. It wouldn't be right to stay here. He'd tell everybody at work that I let my sister run my life.'

'I don't want you to go with him, Michael,' I pleaded. 'You'll have an accident.'

At this point, if it had been one of Michael's old friends, they would have stayed. But Andrew insisted on going.

I walked to the front door with them and kissed Michael. As the car started to move down our drive, panic seized me. I ran after it, screaming, 'Michael, get out of the car! You'll be killed!'

Michael opened his door to get out, but Andrew took off too quickly.

I ran inside, hysterically begging Bob to give me the car keys so I could follow them.

'No,' Bob said, 'it's only a few minutes' drive to his place – he'll be all right.'

I went to bed and dreamed that Michael was tumbling through the air. He was surrounded by a black fog and his new white jumper looked so out of place in all the darkness.

꧁꧂

We had arranged a few weeks earlier to go fishing with friends the next morning. It was a Sunday and, because of my illness through the week, I had forgotten. At 7 o'clock the doorbell rang and it was them. As I let them in, I asked if they had listened to the radio news that morning.

'Yes,' they replied.

'Was there an accident anywhere around here? I'm so worried about Michael – he never carries any identification on him.'

'No, there was nothing like that,' they said, and I went in and dressed. We drove to our fishing spot.

As I got out of the car, though, something happened that I had only experienced once before, when my mother was seriously ill. It is difficult to put into words. But I can only say that it transcended my conscious, reasoning mind, leaving me full of the knowledge of what I had to do. The others were unloading the stuff out of the car when I asked if anyone had change for the phone.

'Why?'

'Just give it to me.'

'But there aren't any phones around here.'

'I'll find one. My brother's dead.' Then I ran and they followed. I reached a public phone and rang information.

'What's the number for the local police station?' I got the number and called it, saying, 'My name is Margaret Dent, my brother's name is Michael Alheit. Have you been trying to locate me?'

'Yes,' said a voice.

'He's dead, isn't he?'

'Yes . . .'

'Please don't send anyone to my mum's house,' I said. 'She's a chronic asthmatic – I'll tell her.'

'I'm sorry, Mrs Dent, but your brother had no identification and we've only in the last hour got his name from the driver of the vehicle. We've just sent an officer to your mum's home.'

'Have you contacted my sister-in-law?' I asked.

'No.'

'I'll do it. I'll go to the hospital and then I'll come to the police station.'

When I walked into the hospital, Ann was sitting up feeding the baby. She took one look at me and burst into tears.

'It's Michael, isn't it?'

'Yes,' I replied.

'Is he dead?'

I nodded.

'I don't want to stay here,' Ann cried.

'I'll take you with me, Ann,' I said.

Bob came in and took the baby. Ann and I clung to each other.

❦

Four minutes after Michael and Andrew had left my house, they were involved in a head-on collision in our road. Andrew's car was on the wrong side of the road, and there were two people in the other car – a girl and her fiancé. The girl was killed; the young man was badly injured and suffered permanent damage to his leg. Andrew sustained a number of injuries.

My brother Michael died in the arms of a girl I sometimes drove to work, though at the time she didn't know he was my brother. The accident happened right outside her house. It was a great comfort to me to learn that his last minutes were not alone, and that he had the support of someone kind and caring.

❦

But my guilt was uncontrollable. No one could ease it or pacify me. I felt it was all my fault. I was angry with myself, and I was angry with Bob for stopping me from going after them. I didn't believe the detective who told me Michael had died quickly; I knew that in my dream Michael was screaming for help.

It was the worst day of my life and I wanted to punish myself. I kept thinking of all the people I had helped, and yet I couldn't help my own brother. Nothing anyone said could break through the wall of anger and guilt. I couldn't even comfort our mum or Ann.

That night – Sunday – Ann, Bob and I were sitting in the lounge room. I had been crying and raving ever since we left the police station. That's how they saw it. One minute I was crying and the next my attention was taken by a light that appeared in the corner of the room. I saw my great-grandfather and, standing beside him, surrounded by beautiful light, was Michael!

The air was suddenly full of a peace that engulfed the whole room. Nothing existed except this wonderful stillness.

Then Michael said, 'You hypocrite!'

I was stunned and didn't understand, but his meaning became clear very quickly. 'You tell people there is no death, you talk about God and you preach faith. You don't believe in God.'

'I do,' I cried. 'How can you say that?'

'You're the one who's telling everyone it was your fault, how you could have prevented my death. So that makes you God, doesn't it? Margaret, I don't know why this happened and I don't like the fact that it did, because my life was just beginning. I had the job I wanted, I had two sons – the baby just three days old – and I love my wife. Yet somehow, I know it's alright. I always knew somewhere inside myself that I would never be old. I'm not saying I knew it would be now, or like this, but here I am and here you all are. I know that you and Mum will look after Ann and the boys. Please tell Mum I love her, too.'

At this point, Ann interrupted: 'Ask him who I have to contact at his work and get the phone number.'

Michael gave me a name and number and Ann wrote them down as I relayed them to her. Then Michael gave us details of the various insurance schemes he had joined and told us who to contact. He gave a message for Ann, explaining that it would be foolish to go back to live in their flat. Next, he asked Bob to attend to some things for him and said, 'I want to help Andrew. Don't hate him and don't blame him.'

There was a lot more about Andrew and, because of Michael, none of us could keep the hate in our hearts afterwards. So much comfort was given to us from Michael that it gave us all the strength and courage to face the days ahead.

It was then that I realised what had happened to me during those four days of sleep. I understood that Michael's death was part of his plan in life and part of the evolution of everyone who was touched by his life. The stage had been set and everything had gone ahead the way the director, God, had written it.

I realised that, had I been awake, I would have tuned in to what was about to happen to Michael and so I was put out of action. When it was time for my role to be played, I was tuned in at once. Let me add that the police station I rang that day was not the one in our own suburb, nor even in the suburb where Michael lived. How did I know where to ring? How did I know Michael was dead? No thought before action; just action.

༄

Michael, like myself, had attended Catholic schools and the funeral service was at the church near where Mum lived. It was the most dreadful service I have ever attended. Because of Michael's age, there were many young people in the congregation and they, like the older people, were all very upset, especially since he had died so tragically. Ann, Bob and I were alright. I had talked to Michael that morning and we knew he would be watching the whole thing. Mum and my grandparents, however, were distraught. It was a terrible ordeal for them.

The priest was elderly, with a thick Irish accent. Sitting there that day, I promised myself that some day, somehow, I would do something about people like this man. He was supposed to be God's representative on earth, to offer comfort and help to the family and friends, to give them something to take away with them – an assurance that Michael was with God. He gave them nothing.

From the time he opened his mouth, no one could understand a word he said. He gave the impression that all he wanted was to get this tiresome job over and done with so he could go and have his breakfast. Without exception, he depressed everyone. Even the funeral director was upset and said so openly when he learned our feelings about death.

I had no idea at the time, but all this opened a way for certain events in the future when I would indeed be in a position to do something about people who looked on funerals as just another job. All I knew then was that I would never again allow a loved one or friend to be in a situation like the one we were in that day.

In time, I realised that the priest, when he passed over, would be able to see the effect of his attitude on others and be a very sorry man. What a shock when he found himself attending his own funeral! This knowledge was enough for me, and I bear him no malice now. He, too, was part of my development, and the words 'every man is my teacher' rang in my head then as they do today.

⁓

The proof of Michael's survival beyond death came as no surprise to me – I had already felt that. It was the release from guilt which followed this knowledge that sustained me, and gave me clarity and direction. This was Michael's gift to me, and to thousands of others. It was at this point that I understood I must dedicate my life to passing on to others the comfort and understanding I had gained from Michael's death.

When we have the sure and certain knowledge of the continued existence of the soul after death, there is a difference that radiates from us when we speak of it. It comes from a faith founded on proof, a proof I have helped others find.

This is my main reason for writing *Love Never Dies* – to help others find this knowledge, and the comfort that comes with it. In Part 1, I will explain what it was like growing up with psychic abilities – how they affected my life, and the lives of those around me, and how I slowly came to terms with being 'different'. These early chapters talk about some of the astonishing events that led me to my teaching, and my work as a medium, both face to face with individuals and large groups, and on the radio.

Through my work and personal experiences, I have been given many lessons and messages, and I believe that many people are now seeking this kind of information. So in Part 2, I will pass on some of what I have learned about spirits, the spirit world, psychic awareness and abilities, and how we can apply these things in our lives to the benefit of all.

PART 1

MY JOURNEY

1

GROWING UP DIFFERENT

VERY FEW PEOPLE, apart from my immediate family, know the stories from my early childhood, but truth can sometimes be stranger than fiction. It now seems I have been waiting all my life for the right time to speak, for a time when I can talk openly and honestly with the public about the things I see and experience. And I still pray for a time when all can be shared and, most importantly, understood.

I am often asked when I became psychic. The truth is that the gift was with me from birth. In fact, many of us carry these abilities part-way through childhood and then lose our capacity to reach out to the world of spirit because we are not encouraged to do so. I was very lucky to have parents who, while not necessarily understanding my spirit needs, nurtured them.

People are continually asking me about my first psychic experiences and my earliest recollections. My earliest memories date from my third birthday.

I lived with my parents in an old house, and my great-aunt, whom I called Nanna, also lived with us. On my third birthday, I was presented with a very expensive gift – a gold bracelet consisting of two tiny hearts with a ruby set in each. My great-aunt, having no children of her own, had kept it all those years to give to her favourite niece's daughter, and today was the long-awaited day. I was told I could only wear this precious bracelet on special occasions.

I didn't enjoy that present. It seemed to me that every time I was having fun playing with the other children, someone would call me into the house to show one of the adults my bracelet. I didn't want to be singled out like that; I just wanted to be one of the crowd. In fact, I was much happier with the simple gifts brought by the children who came to my party.

I remember vividly the emotions I felt all that day. They were confusing and conflicting, involving responsibility and jealousy – not on the part of the children, but of the adults.

By the time the cake arrived, I was in the bathroom being sick. Then, still feeling awful, I was forced to stand in front of all those people – on display again – while happy birthday was sung and the candles were blown out. Of course, I had behaved in a manner that was considered naughty, so when the last guest departed I was sent to bed earlier than usual and the bracelet was put on my bedside table.

Next morning the bracelet was missing. The general opinion was that I had hidden it. I knew I had not. They searched everywhere, but it was nowhere to be found.

Now, I had a friend called Mary. One night, not long after the bracelet had disappeared, I was about to fall asleep when Mary spoke to me. She was standing beside my bed, and she said, 'I know where your bracelet is and I will show you.'

I followed her into the kitchen and she took me to the icebox.

'It is in the mouse hole behind there,' she said.

It so happened my parents were in the kitchen at the time and wanted to know what I was doing out of bed at that hour. I tried to tell them, pointing to the icebox. Well, you can imagine the response that brought. I was marched off to bed, in trouble again.

I tried again the next day but, faced with the same reaction, I gave up. Twelve months later we moved house and when the furniture was taken out of the kitchen, there was the hole behind the icebox. And that's where Dad found the bracelet.

Mary, my first guide, was a little older than me, and no one else could see her because she was a spirit. She had brownish curly shoulder-length hair, brown eyes and was always a little bit taller than me. From the age of three, whenever I saw her, she was wearing an empire-line frock tied at the front with a ribbon. In those days, Mary was a constant companion. I never thought to question her about the fact that she dressed differently from me. I was a tomboy; Mary was always a proper little girl with her dresses, and her hair all neat and tidy, sometimes held back with a ribbon.

Mary and I often sat in the garden, playing and talking. We had wonderful adventures together and shared many secret places that the adults did not know about. Mum always brought a cup for Mary when she brought me a drink, and there was always a cake or sandwich for her too. I didn't know then that I was the only one who could see Mary, but the wonderful thing was that adults in my family never made me feel there was anything strange or different about my playmate. In this I was blessed.

In talking about Mary, I must emphasise that my having a guide doesn't make me unusual, let alone unique. As we'll discuss later, most children have their own experiences with guides, whether they be of human or animal form. Too many parents write off these constant childhood companions as imaginary playmates, when it would be more helpful to respect and acknowledge them.

At this stage of my life I'd no idea that adults didn't tend to have the same experiences. There were, however, experiences that I didn't understand and that I needed help with.

I can remember when I was still quite small being afraid of going to our outside toilet, particularly after dark. Whenever I had to go at night I'd turn on all the lights, then run across the yard as fast as I could. I'd never linger in the toilet because I could see a man (in spirit) hanging there. Once my dad realised there was a problem, he explained that even if somebody had hung themselves in the toilet, all I was seeing was the memory of what had happened. By talking commonsense to me, my dad took away my fear. He helped me to understand that I was seeing the imprint of something that had happened before, not the actual event.

∽

So many events shaped my life in my third year. I am sure there must have been happy ones, but the ones that are indelibly etched in my memory are the ones that caused me anguish, pain and confusion.

Mum, I learned, was expecting a baby. It wasn't Mum who told me, it was Mary. 'It's going to be a boy,' Mary said. When I told Mum I was going to have a baby brother, she said I had to be patient – a phrase I came to hate and dread all through my life. It seemed each day was an eternity. I would ask Mum, 'Is it time? When will he be here?' I always got the same reply, 'Not yet.'

Then I started to worry that the baby might change his mind, that he might not want to be my brother. I couldn't express these thoughts to the adults, but I must have driven them crazy with my constant questions about when the baby would arrive.

I woke one morning to a beautiful day. The sun was shining brightly through my bedroom window and, as I was about to go to my parents' room to wake them up, I became aware of a strange feeling. I couldn't feel my brother around any more. It was as though something had been taken from me. What I did feel was the physical pain of Mum's miscarriage in my own stomach, as well as her grief and confusion. I panicked and ran to my parents' room.

My dad caught me before I could go into the bedroom.

'No,' he said, 'Mummy is sick and the doctor is with her.'

'Why?' I asked.

'It's the flu,' he replied.

All I knew was that there was something wrong with my baby, but I didn't connect Mum's flu with what was wrong. I started screaming that I wanted Mum and had to get into her bedroom to persuade my brother to stay, and that the horrible man they called a doctor was upsetting the baby and causing him to go away.

I was uncontrollable. My dad picked me up and gave me to

my aunt, who kept me outside until my grandparents arrived and took me away for the day. When I came back that night they still wouldn't let me into the bedroom to see Mum, but they promised I could see her the next day. I tried to convince myself that the reason I could not feel my brother around was because he was in the room with Mum.

When I saw her the next morning I was so happy she was feeling better – but as she held me in her arms, I knew my brother was not there. I started to cry and asked where he was and what had happened. My dad carried me out and, for a long time, I was angry with Mum because I believed I could have talked the baby into staying if they had let me into the bedroom earlier.

I can't say exactly when, but these thoughts changed into ones of self-doubt, and they stayed with me for many years. Being as young as I was, all I could think was, 'It's my fault. He didn't want me, I must have done something wrong.' It was Mary who helped to calm me down. She let me know Mum was all right and she told me the baby would be back.

Over the years I've come to understand there are many reasons for miscarriages. Naturally one must take into account the health of the mother, but there's more to it than that. Often the soul only needs a short amount of time back in this earth dimension to complete its cycle of growth. In these cases the soul was never meant to be born into this world.

Sadly mothers think they're being punished when they lose a baby, when in fact it's an agreement made between the mother and the other soul before either incarnates. It's a pact made for their mutual enlightenment and growth. If only more mothers understood this, what a difference it would make.

Life continued on. Mum told me I would be going to pre-school one day a week. I was so excited – all those children to play with, and the swings and slippery dip. I could hardly wait.

But I hated the first day. My teacher made me leave my floral case outside, and I couldn't understand why Mary wasn't with me. We had to drink milk, which I hated, and promptly brought back up. Worse, the other children wouldn't let me get on the swings and slippery dip I had so looked forward to. This was the first time in my life that I experienced peer group cruelty. I was the new girl, the outsider.

The next week, I kicked and screamed. The teacher assured Mum that every child was the same and that I would soon settle in. I can still remember that day. The teacher was annoyed because I wanted to take my floral case into the playroom with me. I couldn't make her understand that I was panicking because I thought I was going to lose it.

As the morning went on, we were all informed that a very naughty child had stolen an article from one of the other children's bags. Teacher said that unless someone owned up, no one would be allowed outside to play. I didn't know why, but I felt guilty and it was a relief when she searched all our cases because I half expected the stolen article to turn up in my precious case. The culprit turned out to be a little boy, but the guilt I felt that day was stronger than logic. In fact, I had been picking up the boy's feelings of guilt, but was too young to realise or understand what was happening. When we were let out to play I sneaked back inside, collected my case and left preschool.

As I was trying to find my way home I became aware of a man's voice. I did not see him, and only many years later put a face to the much loved voice of Chang Tao, who became my guide and companion. When I reached the main road, I did as Chang told me and asked a lady if I could walk across the road with her. With more instructions from Chang, I found my way safely home.

Mum didn't make me go back to preschool. From then on, Nanna looked after me while Mum and Dad were at work.

ॐ

In 1950, when I was four years old, we moved house. Mum was in hospital because my new baby brother had been born, and a friend of Mum's was taking care of me. When we arrived at the new house, she told me Mum would be home later that day.

Every time I asked Mum's friend a question about the baby, she said, 'It all depends. Be a good girl and go out and play.' How could I? I was going through hell. What if my brother changed his mind again and didn't want to stay? I couldn't make her or anyone else understand. Not only was I experiencing a recurrence of the fears I had been through twelve months earlier, but I was also frightened Mary might not be able to find our new house.

When Nanna arrived, I talked to her about my fears. 'I will put your tea set on the back veranda with Mary's cup, and you can sit and wait for her. I'm sure she'll be here,' she said.

She was right. Along came Mary, and my world was coming into balance again.

It was decided that my brother would be named Michael. I knew then, as I know now, that this was the same soul that my Mum had miscarried in the previous pregnancy.

And I was aware, for all the twenty-four years of Michael's life, that he felt a certain reluctance to be on the earth plane. This doesn't mean he was in any way suicidal – far from it. But from the beginning, everyone commented on how much this baby slept. I was forever trying to wake him up, thinking he didn't want to stay here and that he really wanted to go back.

As Michael began to grow, we realised that he had problems with his speech and he was a slow walker. Mum consulted so many specialists and always came away with the same answers. Nothing is wrong with him – he is a fat baby, he is slow, he will walk and talk when he is ready. I never worried about these things. I just accepted this was Michael, but I did worry constantly about his sleeping, in case he decided to leave us.

Michael was impossible to wake, and if you didn't take the time to wake him slowly, his whole body would stiffen, his eyes would open and stare blankly at you, and then he would scream and scream. Needless to say, the household would try to keep everything quiet when he was sleeping, so as not to wake him prematurely.

From the day he started walking, my problems about his sleeping became a nightmare. He and I shared our bedroom with our great-aunt. She had a single bed on one side of our large bedroom and Michael and I had bunk beds. I had to sleep on the top bunk because, from the time he started to walk, Michael sleepwalked.

I remember the first time. It was the very early hours of the morning, and I awoke with a start because the front doorbell was ringing. I leaned over, ready to grab Michael in case I had to hold him down – something I had become used to doing if he was startled.

But Michael wasn't there. I jumped out of bed and ran into the hallway with Mum, just as Dad was opening the front door. A neighbour, Mr Hill, was standing there holding Michael's hand. Mr Hill told my parents that he had been on his way to work when he came across Michael walking up the road. He questioned him but got no answer.

I started crying. I can still remember the blank look in Michael's eyes, staring straight through me and totally unaware of his surroundings. Mum comforted me while Dad picked Michael up and took him back to bed, tucking the covers over him.

Later, Mum told me Michael had been sleepwalking and from now on we would have to make sure the front and back doors were securely locked so he could not get out of the house. Dad said he had encountered this before – someone walking in their sleep. I remember Dad impressing on me that it was important not to wake Michael up, just get him back to bed.

I can't count the times Michael got out of the house sleep-walking, nor the number of times the police were involved in looking for him. We had locks on the side gate, the front gate, the front door and the wire door. The windows were locked, but still he got out. He learnt to climb through a hole in our side fence and out through our neighbour's front gate.

One weekend there was an episode I remember so clearly. It was to be the last of Michael's sleepwalking escapades. I woke up, leaned over to check, and he was gone. The bedroom window was open. I woke Nanna, then ran into my parents' room to alert them. We all went separate ways searching, but when we met back at the house, no one had found him.

I sat on the back step, worried, when a voice from spirit said to me, 'Look in the park.' I answered, 'He couldn't be there because they lock the park every night, and it's still too early for it to be open.' The voice repeated, 'Look in the park.'

The park was a block away from our house. It was small, with swings, a slippery dip and a merry-go-round, and it was surrounded by a high wall. I stopped arguing with the voice and told Dad where I was going. He had the same arguments as I had, but finally he said, 'Alright, but come straight back.'

When I arrived at the park, as I expected, the gate was locked. I had started to walk away when I heard a familiar sound: the noise of a swing moving back and forth. Sure enough, there at the side of the fence was a hole – and in the park, swinging backwards and forwards, was Michael.

A mixture of relief and anger surged in me, but I controlled myself and said calmly, 'Michael.' I don't know how many times I called his name, hoping he would stop the dangerous swinging. I was terribly afraid of waking him up, but how else was I going to get him off the swing? I gave up and sat on the grass crying until I heard Dad's voice asking, 'How did you get into the park?'

I told him about the hole in the wall, but it was too small for him to get through. He kept talking to me from the other side of the fence, and I kept crying, never letting my eyes leave Michael on the swing.

Later – I don't know how much later – a policeman, Dad, and the man with the park key came through the gate. I still remember their faces as they stood there, watching my brother having a great time playing on the swing. Fast asleep.

Michael and I started sleeping together in the bottom bunk. I don't know if that was the reason, but he never sleepwalked again. Still, for the rest of his life we had to be careful how he was woken up.

Sleeping together brought new problems, one of which was being told by our parents and Nanna to stop talking or fighting and go to sleep. He would be tucked into bed for the night, and then he would start: 'I hate . . .'

Whenever I heard those words I would cringe, because I knew he wouldn't stop. It might be, 'I hate those lines.'

'What lines? There aren't any lines.' I would say.

'There is so.'

'But the walls have no lines.'

'The lines have big eyes.'

And then I would understand. Lions. Michael was seeing spirit animals. So, that was it. Now I could try and help, or so I thought. I tried to explain that there was nothing to worry about, that the shapes and eyes we could see in the dark wouldn't hurt us. But it made no difference. Michael hated them and wanted to know why I didn't make them go away. The end result would be me having a nightmare because his fear was catching and overrode my commonsense.

⤷⤶

For as long as I can remember I have never considered death something to be afraid of, because I have always known where people go when they die. It has always been quite normal for me to talk to those in spirit, and it was only in my teen years that I began to think there was something wrong with me.

Certainly, I found out at an early age that others could not see and hear what I could. This was a very lonely time for me, as it is for any child who has such gifts. Even today we adults tend to underestimate how much nurturing such kids need. In retrospect, I believe I owe my sanity to a strong will and a sense of humour. And to the supportive understanding of my parents.

I attended the local Catholic school where the nuns were very old, and the majority were short on patience. I was always in trouble, getting the cane and being kept back after school. I wasn't beyond running home when things got too much for me either.

The biggest problem with school, however, was that I was forever talking to dead nuns and I hadn't learnt to keep my mouth shut. It wasn't always bad. It depended which living nun was to be the recipient of the message I got. Some said it was the work of the Devil and I had to spend time with the priest; others kept it quiet and sent me to the Mother Superior.

A lot of these episodes confused other children. They didn't understand why I was always in trouble, because it was never discussed openly. Looking back, I realise that the nuns who always picked on me were the ones who were most afraid of me. Thank God for the ones who cared. They understood when I walked out of school because I felt I had been unjustly treated or accused.

I remember the Mother Superior fondly. It was only years later that I realised just how much she protected me. I would often sit with her in the nuns' garden after school, and these are times I treasure in memory. Of course, she wanted me to become a nun, but although I was very religious and went to church from love, not duty, my sense of humour kept getting me into trouble and it seems I spent years of my life on my knees reciting Hail Marys or doing the stations of the cross as penance.

All through these years, the voice of Chang Tao (my guide who first spoke to me when I was three) was with me, as all our guides are, presenting opportunities for me to learn and grow. Because of my gift, our relationship was probably more direct, but it is no different for any of us, as long as we're ready and willing to progress.

Chang would teach me about spiritual principles and practical information at a level I could understand.

I remember I was madly in love with Maggie, the dog that lived in a flat where we were. I used to play with her all the time. 'Why can't she talk and tell me about herself?' I'd ask. The answers would come to me visually and I learned that Maggie was as important as any human and needed the same love and respect. Then, when I went to play in the garden, my guides would tell me not to tread on snails because to do so would be like stepping on Maggie. And so, through these simple examples, I began to learn the interconnectedness of all things.

There were other voices that came and went. Later, I discovered that in spirit there are different teachers for different subjects, just as there are in the school system today. The people I saw and heard, who gave me messages for the nuns, were not spirit teachers, however. They were people who had passed over and wanted to let friends and family know what was happening. These people caused me much trouble at school, but it never occurred to me to say no to them. For me, it was like being surrounded by an unruly crowd all the time. When I needed to block them out, I would deliberately involve myself in other things to keep my mind active.

I was fortunate with my guides, however. They brought with them a wonderful feeling of peace. It was not unusual for my guides to take me to places in their world where I would see wonderful cities, meet people and play in beautiful gardens. I was also shown certain things that were to happen in the future in our world, including medical discoveries such as a non-invasive, non-radioactive diagnostic machine which will replace X-rays and many other current tests.

I had a favourite fantasy, in which I imagined a sort of wheel-barrow with a motor. It was covered in, so I could ride up and down the hill to school in the rain without getting wet. My guide showed me a car of the future. It was nameless then, but turned out to be an exact likeness of a Mini Minor – not so different from the covered wheelbarrow of my dreams.

At this time, one of the biggest problems in the world was Russia. The subject was forever coming up at school. I was told by my guides that the world need not fear Russia as it would become a very religious nation in the future. I was also told not to fear China, that it would not pose a threat to the world.

However, it was instilled in me by my guides that what the world really had to fear was religious intolerance and natural disasters. Between the ages of five and ten I was taught a great deal about weather patterns and was shown how, in my lifetime, there would be major changes in the cycles of the seasons and an increase in erratic weather. I was even shown snow in places where, at that time, people didn't experience a frost.

≈

At school, whenever I was not interested in the lesson, I would drift off into the spirit world dimensions that surround our own. There I would have my own psychic adventures, talking to other beings, getting lessons from them. My concentration could easily be in two or more places at once, which was a great appren-ticeship for my mediumship.

I know now that this is a process called shifting of consciousness, where one receives impressions through the subconscious
mind, bypassing the conscious mind. At the time, I didn't bother
to examine this process too closely because I believed everyone
had the same experiences as me. It was only years later that I
realised this was not the case. However, I didn't share this part
of my existence with children of my own age, as I had learnt
early on that they would think I was weird.

My mum said that although I was forever surrounded by other
children, I was also on the outer, and so I was always lonely. I
gave the appearance of being a happy, well-adjusted child, a
ringleader with a mature nature, and quite often the clown of
the group. People excused my escapades, especially those connected with school, as a moodiness they could sometimes see in
my nature. My parents didn't think of me as moody – they knew
exactly why I behaved as I did. Well, they may not have completely understood, but they tried.

My mum said I got into a lot of my trouble because I was
too truthful, doing things in front of people instead of behind
their backs. Some may think this is an excellent attribute, but
sometimes it's not. More often than I could count, I asked myself
why I was so stupid. By the time I reached high school I had
learnt to shut up, but this caused me even more problems. There
were always compensations, however, and opportunities to learn.

Occasionally I used to walk to school with a girl named
Rhonda, who lived in the street next to ours. We had a funny
relationship – going to the same school was about all we had in
common.

She was reserved and always neat and tidy. We never walked
home together, we didn't mix in the same crowd at school and
I never saw her in the parks where most of the children played.
Her hair was black, longer than mine, and it always amazed me
that she never had a hair out of place. At the end of the day,
her ribbons were always still perfectly tied to her perfectly plaited
hair, and her hat looked as if it had just come out of the hatbox.
My hair, on the other hand, was always getting me into trouble.
The knots and tangles caused a screaming match every morning,

with Mum rushing to leave for work, trying to plait my flyaway blond hair.

I had never been inside Rhonda's house. Mostly we met at her front gate. If I was taking Michael to school we would meet at the bottom of her street. Her house was the largest in the street. It was newly built and stood out amongst the others.

One morning she was not at the gate when I arrived. I waited until I began to feel agitated about being late for school, then I walked up to the front door and knocked. Mrs Walters, Rhonda's mum, answered the door. 'Come in,' she said. I followed her into the lounge room and sat down to wait.

It was the most enormous lounge room I had ever seen. I felt nervous and uncomfortable, and didn't understand why I wanted to run. I thought it must be because I was going to be late for school, but when I looked at the clock on the mantelpiece, I could see I still had plenty of time. I was thinking, 'If I walk out the front door now, they'll tell everyone how rude I am.' My mind was driving me crazy, and I was close to panicking.

Then Mrs Walters and Rhonda appeared in the doorway. Mrs Walters said, 'Rhonda's grandmother is sick in bed with the flu, and when she heard you were here she asked if you'd come and say hello. She has always liked you, Margaret.'

With my mouth I said, 'Yes,' but with my mind I thought, 'But I don't even know her grandmother.'

They led me to the biggest bedroom I had ever been in, with a fire burning in an open fireplace and, opposite it against the other wall, an enormous dressing table. There were huge bay windows with velvet curtains that reminded me of our local picture show. In the middle of the room was a bed that looked twice the size of Mum and Dad's double bed, and in the middle was a lady sitting propped up by pillows all around her. Her dark, greying hair was piled up on top of her head, without a hair out of place.

I recognised her as a Mrs Bell, someone I had often talked to in the local shop. Of course, I should have realised she was Rhonda's grandmother because her hair was always perfectly groomed. I stood away from the bed, just inside the door.

'Come closer,' she said.

'How can I?' I thought. I had never seen so many people crammed into a bedroom before. The panic started again and my mind was screaming, 'Who is real, who do I say excuse me to, and who do I walk right through?' Now I understood why I had wanted to run when I was in the lounge room. A lot of these people were in old-fashioned clothes and I reasoned that they were spirits. But that still left quite a few others in question.

'Sit on the bed, Margaret,' the old lady said.

'Well, here goes,' I thought, and sat next to a woman who was sitting close to Mrs Bell's head.

Everyone seemed to be talking at the same time. I was aware of a darkness coming from around Mrs Bell's head. All I wanted to do was get out of that house. I have no idea what I said, but I remember rushing from the front gate all the way to school, with Rhonda saying, 'We won't be late, there's still plenty of time.' I desperately wanted to ask her how many people there were in the bedroom, but I was afraid to.

After school I went and sat in the church. I didn't understand what was happening, and so I prayed for Mrs Bell. It was a Friday, and all weekend I was troubled. I just couldn't understand why so many spirit people would be gathered in a bedroom. And what was that blackness? I had never seen anything like that before. I was angry with myself for not thinking to ask one of the spirit people about all this, but at the time I had been confused and only wanted to get out.

On the Monday, I decided not to call past Rhonda's house. When I arrived at school, I was told that Rhonda would not be at school that day because her grandmother had passed away on Saturday with a heart attack. I was so distressed. Could I have done something? Was I supposed to tell Mrs Bell about those people? Nobody had given me a message – in fact, they didn't even seem to notice me.

I went through hell all that day, and after school I went to Rhonda's house. I didn't go inside, I just sat on their brick fence. I don't know why. I felt I had to know if Mrs Bell was alright and, of course, no one alive could give me that information. It started to get late, nothing was happening, and I felt like an idiot. How could I explain why I was sitting on the fence if anyone asked me? Not to mention the trouble I would be in for getting home late from school.

I was just about to get off the fence when a voice said, 'Hello, Margaret.' It was Mrs Bell. She was surrounded by a beautiful blue-white light – gone was that awful blackness that had been engulfing her when I had last seen her.

I quickly realised she was not alone, and I recognised the lady standing with her as the one I had seen sitting on her bed. There was also a man, whom I vaguely remembered seeing. Mrs Bell told me he was her husband who had died many years before, and the other lady was her mother.

'Are you alright?' I asked.

'Yes, I am very happy,' she replied.

'Mrs Bell, what was that blackness all around you?'

'What blackness? I saw only the most beautiful light, and then the faces of my dead relatives.'

Mrs Bell's mother then said, 'My dear, that is what happens to a person's body when they are approaching death. The life force is leaving the body, since the body has no further use for it, and it's on its way to help the next body – the spirit body.'

This conversation was being carried on through our thoughts, so I didn't have time to think about what she said. Mrs Bell went on to tell me that she was aware of my anxiety after she had died and wanted to put my mind at ease. She said they had been trying for two days to put the thought in my mind that I should come and sit on the fence outside her house. Once again, she assured me that she was alright and thanked me for worrying about her. Then we said our goodbyes.

As I walked home, I became more concerned about being late and pushed the encounter out of my mind. Sure enough, I was in trouble. Mum had wanted me to go to the shop, and I couldn't explain where I had been and what I had been doing.

In bed that night I at last had time to think about the explanation for the blackness I had seen. I couldn't fully comprehend what I had been told, so I was left with a dread of seeing the same thing again in the future – because if I did, I would know that the person was dying.

What I was to learn was that when the life force begins to leave the body, the aura starts to dull. This is the spirit leaving its earth vehicle. When asked what it looks like, I can only say it's a blackness like nothing else we see on earth, it's really the blackness of nothingness. It's nothing sinister and we only see this when a person is very close to death.

I was too young to properly understand then, and it certainly didn't occur to me to tell anyone about my experience. But I did want to tell Rhonda about her grandmother so she would not be so upset. I struggled mentally between telling her and running the risk of ridicule, or not telling her. At times I felt I should, and at other times I was so afraid that I stayed away from her.

When she came back to school I would say hello, but I never called at her house again. I was sorry I couldn't trust myself, even when all the other children went to her and said how sorry they were about her grandmother. I just had to keep away. I asked for guidance from my spirit friends and was told it was best for me to make my own decisions.

Things were becoming increasingly complicated for me. I was finding that the children I had as friends seemed to be growing away from me. It was difficult at home, and when I was invited to sleep overnight at a friend's house, I couldn't. I tried, but I would be so worried about Mum's terrible asthma and about Michael that I would then want to go home, and this would upset my friend's parents. Naturally, I couldn't tell them the real reason for not staying, and my made-up excuses just sounded stupid.

I didn't want to go back to the same school, so Mum enrolled me in another Catholic college, in fact the same school she had attended. Despite my wonderful teacher, Sister Haskell, life at school still wasn't easy. I was eleven now, and I was having difficulty coming to terms with the teachings of the church – so much of what had been revealed to me was against Catholic teaching. Of course, this had always been true, but it was getting worse as I grew older.

Once, during class, I drew a picture. It was a view of a country landscape as seen from the sky. This drawing was confiscated by my teacher because I was supposed to be doing a maths assignment at the time and I was accused of daydreaming. First the teachers, and then the principal, made a great deal of fuss about this drawing. I made the mistake of telling them I could fly and this was one of my favourite views from the air. I didn't know then that there was a name for what I was doing, which is astral travelling. It was something Michael and I had great fun doing together. We would go to the tops of houses or anywhere we wanted to look at the views.

So when I talked at school about flying, I was telling the nuns the truth as I knew it – I could fly and always had. But Mum was called up to the school, and once again I was sent over to the church to do the usual Hail Marys and stations of the cross as penance after a talk with the parish priest.

The best thing about my new school was my teacher, Sister Haskell. She was a wonderful help and encouraged my spiritual development in a way I had not experienced before. One day I told her that I loved hearing the nuns singing, and asked her why we didn't see all the nuns in school. 'There must be a lot of nuns living in the convent,' I said, 'because when I hear the singing, all the nuns I know who teach me are still in the playground.'

She questioned me about the hymns they were singing, and I gave her the names of the ones that I recognised, hummed the tunes of some that weren't familiar to me, and told her all the singing was done in Latin.

Sister Haskell invited me to sit with her in the garden next morning, and this was especially exciting to me since the nuns' garden was out of bounds to the students, and the nuns' chapel was in the garden. We sat on a bench, just opposite the chapel.

This became a common practice for us, one that continued until I left school. I could hear the most beautiful voices singing, sometimes solo, and sometimes as a choir. Sister Haskell would ask me to talk about the singing and what I was hearing. After a few of these sessions over about three weeks, she told me that when we sat there listening, there were no earthly nuns singing in the chapel. She had gone through the convent records and discovered that the times I had heard the voices were consistent with the schedule of the convent many years before. She was even able to put names to the hymns I could not recognise. Some of them were no longer sung in the convent, but all had previously been sung only by nuns and not taught to the pupils.

Sister Haskell said that during the years she had spent in this convent, she and others had heard this same phenomenon from time to time, but now, sitting in the garden with me, she had heard more than before and would sometimes hear the whole hymn from beginning to end.

When I was eleven, we moved house again and I had to travel a long distance from home to school, which made it difficult to sustain friendships outside school hours. I hated being cooped up in four walls, so the travelling suited me. For variety, I would stay at my grandparents' house, where I could go swimming or do things with school friends. At school, I played the role of comedian. I didn't speak to anyone about my life, my voices or my spirit friends at this time. I isolated myself from the physical world a great deal and drew closer to the unseen worlds.

Ever since I was three years old, my guides have taught me in three distinct ways. When I was a small child, they read stories to me. As I grew older, things that were taught at school would trigger questions, and my guides supplied the answers. During the first six years at school, these questions were mainly gener-ated by religious teachings that bothered me. Thirdly, to teach me about history, my guides would take me astrally to places where I could watch particular events as they happened. This was like being at a live performance rather than watching a replay on television. I never questioned this process. As far as I was concerned at the time, it was normal. Describing this process now as an adult, I can only say that for all intents and purposes, I was an onlooker at that time in the past.

Mum and Dad had recently separated, adding to my traumas. I was very afraid that someone at school would find out, and my sense of guilt was unbelievable. I believed I must have done something very wrong for this to have happened. But once again my saviour was my sense of humour and my ability to laugh.

Michael was making his own friends and becoming involved with his own interests. We still did things together, but ours was no longer the inseparable companionship we had shared for the past ten years. What I didn't realise at this stage was that this development was quite normal. His spiritual eyes were closing and he could no longer join in the things we had shared spiritually.

Looking back, I can't blame Michael. Kids want to fit in and be like everyone else. There's a price attached to nurturing our spiritual self and not everyone feels ready to pay it. At the time, though, I was overwhelmed with sadness to see Michael becoming less and less interested in listening to his inner voice.

Up until this time we'd spoken about unusual things we each saw and experienced, and that kept Michael's spiritual sensitivities alive. As he moved away from spiritual understandings, and mixed more and more with his mates, Michael hardened. He took on other peoples' values, and began to deny the wider experiences that had come to him, until eventually his gifts became little more than a dim memory.

The interesting thing is, you can actually see this happening to a person. The aura of a compassionate person is pink, and indicates a level of understanding that tends to be beyond their years and experience in this present life. A less compassionate person has a smaller showing of a paler pink in their aura. We have to use our gifts, spiritual and otherwise, or they leave us.

I have since learned that all children's spiritual eyes are opened at the time of their birth, but because of their parents' beliefs and their environment, they have to become part of this world and the memories fade. They lose their awareness, and the scenes from the spirit world grow dull, until all that is left are vague experiences that are attributed to their imagination.

It always strikes me as funny that so many people then spend the rest of their lives trying to open their spiritual eyes again, when sadly we help shut the spiritual eyes of our children by the way we react to them.

As a kid I enjoyed sports, and particularly tennis. Tennis was my passion. When I was not playing on the school tennis court, I would hit the ball against the wall of an electricity sub-station across the road from where we lived. This was my outlet, and I understand now what I got out of the many hours I spent hitting those tennis balls. It was a form of meditation that would prove invaluable in my work as a medium in the years ahead.

When I was hitting the tennis ball my concentration never faded, and at the same time my spirit friends were easily able to communicate with me because of my receptive state of mind.

There was one competition tennis match I had been looking forward to for weeks, but never got to play in. I left home in my new white tennis dress and was sitting on the first of the two buses I had to catch when I started to feel sick. I didn't take much notice of my nausea because I suffered from motion sickness. But then I began to feel hot, very hot. A pain racked my whole body until I was doubled over. I knew something was horribly wrong so I caught another bus to where Mum worked.

She called a taxi to take me to hospital, and they operated at once, removing my appendix. I didn't recover as quickly as I should have and spent three months off school. The enormous impact of this illness was unbearable for me.

I was devastated at not being able to play tennis and the limitations of being housebound. At first, the doctor said I was making a slow recovery, but as time passed it became obvious something was amiss. This was to be the first of many such experiences for which the doctors could not find medical answers. Their words would play on my nerves and my imagination would haunt me. My passion for tennis died and I never played again.

When I returned to school I couldn't keep up with the work. To repeat a year was unthinkable, so they arranged extra tuition but, unfortunately, I had lost interest.

Things were financially very difficult at home. Mum was working overtime and had a second job, but we were still close to losing the family home. I decided it would be better for me to be working so I could contribute to our income, and at the same time continue my education at night school. Of course,

Mum didn't want me to do this, but it was obvious that the very idea of school was distressing me so much that I grew sicker and sicker.

And so I left school and went to work.

2

COMING TO TERMS WITH MY PSYCHIC ABILITIES

MY FIRST JOB WAS AS A CASHIER in a grocery store near where I lived. Although I was only fourteen, I told them I was seventeen; this age difference was to help me get other jobs over the next few years.

It was a small store by today's standards, and the three of us who worked there got on very well. I settled in quickly, and loved my job. The customers liked me because I was friendly and listened to their problems. After a while, I became a senior cashier, and was part of the team of troubleshooters who helped out at other branches of the store when they were short of staff.

❧

Not long after I started work I went on an excursion with a group of Michael's friends to the city's big amusement park, Luna Park. We were allowed to go on condition we were home by twelve o'clock. This was a first for us – we had never been to Luna Park at night before. Because two of the group were older than us, we were considered to be in safe hands.

When we boarded the ferry, a lot of ambulance cadets in uniform were also getting on. I don't know why, but I said to one of our group, 'We'll be well looked after if we have an accident on the ferry.' I was told to shut up and control my warped sense of humour.

We had a wonderful time at Luna Park, but all too soon we were standing on the wharf waiting for the ferry, the *Emerald Star*, to take us back to the city. We sat in the stern section, which didn't have a roof. The ferry quickly filled with people and, once again, the ambulance cadets were among them.

Everyone was talking and it was very noisy. People were standing and there was absolutely no room left. We were like sardines lined up edge to edge in the can and I was very grateful we were sitting down. The air was full of a feeling of comradeship because everyone had had a good time. We were all of a similar age and were enjoying each other's company.

All of a sudden the noise dulled for me. I became aware of a feeling of not being part of the scene. It was as if I were floating above everything and looking down on my surroundings, rather than being a part of them. I found myself looking down on the boat and the people on it — I could even see myself sitting there.

Out of the darkness a boat appeared. I could tell it was going to hit the *Emerald Star*. Suddenly a voice screamed so loudly that it penetrated through all the other noise. The effect was a shocked silence.

It was my own voice yelling, 'Move to the other side of the boat, we're going to be hit!' I was back in my body, and people were staring at me.

My brother jumped up from his seat and loudly repeated what I had said as he pushed his way to the other side of the boat. My friends followed, as did everyone else in our section. They all had time to get to the other side except me and then, exactly as I had foreseen, the crash happened.

The only difference was that now the people on deck were all on the opposite side of the boat staring out at the blackness when the crash came. Their screams had alerted the passengers inside. Some of them tried to move out, but because the ferry was so crowded they couldn't go anywhere.

The rear section, where we were, received the worst of the impact. The interior damage was mostly from broken glass flying from the windows. I was wedged into a seat by two pieces of wood, one on the left and one on the right. A fraction of an inch either way and I might not be here to tell the story. I was trapped in an upright position with my arms pinned beside me, making it impossible for me to move.

Then Michael was beside me, breaking the wood apart with his hands. 'Why didn't you move when we did? Why? You told everyone else to, why didn't you move?' I couldn't answer him.

More people came to help and they managed to get me free. Michael took me in his arms and that was the last I remembered. The next thing I knew, I was lying on an ambulance stretcher at Circular Quay. I could see the ferry tied up at the wharf. People were being taken away in ambulances. I could see Michael and our friends, but strangers were asking me questions as well.

I was answering without thinking and didn't realise it was the media until Michael told me to be quiet. He looked very upset and didn't want me talking to these strangers. Suddenly it registered on me – the papers, the radio stations. I found out later that all this started because the people in the rear section with me were all talking about how I had shouted my warning well before the actual crash.

'How did you know?'

'How did you manage to see the boat before the other passengers or even the captain saw it?'

'How?'

'Why?'

The questions came thick and fast but, before I understood who was asking them, I had given my full name and even my age.

'Oh, God,' I thought then, 'if Mum hears this she'll have an asthma attack. If my boss hears my real age, I'll be fired.'

I told Michael my fears and he and our friends acted promptly. He travelled in the ambulance with me to hospital and the others caught a taxi to our house. They arrived at the door just as Mum was hearing my name over the radio.

Thank heavens Michael had shut me up. I was still in shock

while I was being questioned, and starting to give details about the boat that had hit us – details I couldn't have known through any normal means.

The story appeared on the front pages of the newspapers next day. I spent three days in bed, and all I remember about those three days is the never-ending motion of the ferry. In my mind I was still on board.

Some months later there was an enquiry into the accident. All the circumstances I'd seen that had led up to the accident were proven to be true.

Not long after the *Emerald Star* incident, my mum was telling me about something that had happened when she was five. I had never seen the house in which she lived at that age, but I interrupted her and began describing it to her. I told her about the toys she'd had, the clothes she wore and even described the furniture in the house.

'How do you know about these things?' she asked me.

'I have watched you,' I answered.

During my visits to the spirit world I had been able to see my mum as a child growing up and, in the course of these experiences, was able to observe the different events that influenced her life. One of my favourite memories of those observations was watching Mum sitting on the front step of her house, daydreaming. When I was three, Mum had taken a photo of me sitting on that very same step at what was my grandparents' place. I guess she saw herself in me, but whenever I see that wonderful photo I remember my mum as the little girl sitting on the step.

I then went on to tell my mum about important happenings at various stages in her life and even gave her a description of another house in which she'd lived as a teenager.

When I had finished speaking, Mum told me that when she was a young girl of about fifteen, an older girlfriend had taken her to have a reading done by a woman named Mrs Johnson. In the course of the reading, this woman told Mum she would have three children. The first would be a girl, the second a boy and the third another girl. According to Mrs Johnson the first child would be gifted and her name would become well known. Well, Mum had only two children at the time we were talking, and for many years afterwards she was convinced that was all the children she'd have.

As for my being gifted – Mum made sure I was taught the piano all through my school days, thinking that 'gifted' and 'well known' could mean through music. When it became painfully obvious that I had no musical talent, she discounted the reading as having been wrong.

But some years later my mum divorced my dad, remarried, and had a baby girl. I, through my mediumship and radio and television appearances, became quite well known, and so Mum had to revise her opinion. Years later, she became my constant support in my work, my buffer against the world, and my secretary.

About this time I was working in a self-service store and had become friends with a girl named Jan, who lived nearby. Jan was a Dutch girl, very nervous and superstitious. We would meet where I worked every Friday and catch a bus or taxi together into the city.

One particular Friday we were in a hurry to get into town to see a show. We began to walk in the direction of the city, watching all the time for a taxi. We had walked quite a distance, and I was a few steps ahead of Jan. We were walking along the main road and I had just passed a big plate glass window and reached the door of a department store. Ahead of me was another window, just as big.

The air was full of the usual street noises and traffic sounds. It was dusk and there weren't many people around. Suddenly, there was complete stillness. I was aware of what was happening, but strangely detached. Another part of me had taken over. There was a sense of knowing what was about to take place, and then I saw a policeman walking towards me, just about to pass the second expanse of glass.

I ran onto the road, screaming out to the policeman, 'There's an explosion!'

The policeman stopped in his tracks. Jan ran out onto the road – and the building exploded! A great ball of fire burst through the front, hurling glass onto the street. The impact threw the policeman to the ground.

Jan was alright, because she had run out and was standing beside me. We both rushed to the policeman. He was bleeding and he had a few cuts, but it was obvious that he, too, was alright. He looked up and said, 'If you hadn't screamed when you did I would have taken the full force of that blast.' Then he gave me a strange look and asked, 'How did you know?'

'I smelt gas,' I told him, though I didn't really know why I had screamed.

'I didn't hear exactly what you called out,' he said, 'but you were so loud that it gave me a fright and I stopped in my tracks.'

I can remember thinking then that one thing I never have a problem with is people hearing me when I raise my voice. I even won a screaming contest at a local cinema when I was a child. Isn't it funny what things go through your mind at deadly serious moments? Thank God for a sense of humour.

Jan had encountered examples of my insight before, but nothing had prepared her for this demonstration of my psychic ability. She was still in shock. She had heard exactly what I had yelled to the policeman, and in her mind I had shown some sort of superhuman power.

During our friendship I had not said much to her about this side of my nature. I realised that she was a girl who was frightened of many things in life, and I had been guarded with her. However, it was impossible to hide it from her all the time, especially when I could see she was making a mistake in judging a person or making a wrong move in life. So I knew the exact moment when our friendship ended. The scene outside the department store was suddenly busy. Fire engines had arrived. Two ambulance officers were treating the policeman, and another one was talking to Jan. As she looked at me, I saw something in her eyes that I have seen many times since.

Jan's eyes transmitted a message of all the age-old fears – fear of the unknown, fear of anything outside normal experience, fear of anything the analytical mind cannot explain. At times like that, people shut it all out of their conscious minds, deciding they don't want to deal with it. It is easier to ignore it because it is too uncomfortable to accept anything that interferes with the belief system.

Jan and I saw each other occasionally after that, but we drifted apart. I clung to all the usual human hopes, as I would do many times with similar friendships through the years. If Jan had really got to know me, I thought, she would have known I was not a bad person, not even different. I was the same as I had always been, and those who spoke to me and guided me were all good people. It wasn't my fault that others couldn't see them or hear them. But I couldn't explain all this to her because I didn't fully understand it myself. I discovered that the more I learnt, the more I had to learn. And I am still learning today.

⁂

The time came when I discovered that boys were more than friends. Then everything changed. I started going out seriously with a boy – I will call him Paul. We had a long relationship and we even became engaged, but our affair was forever on and off. We were good friends. He was a little older than me, very logical and honest.

My mum had remarried and I moved out of the family home soon after. I was still very young and in those days it was considered wrong not to live at home, but I moved out anyway. Michael didn't have the same problems with our new stepfather that I had, and he was happy to stay.

I remember the day I left home, a suitcase in one hand and a bag in the other, walking along the road with not the faintest idea where I was going. And yet, the part of my nature that I could not put a name to filled me with a sense of peace and harmony and told me all was well.

A car pulled up, and Paul's voice called out my name. He had just dropped into our place and Mum had told him what had happened. We sat and talked for a long time until he was convinced I was not returning home. He drove me to his parents' house and told them what had happened, and they insisted I stay with them until I decided what I was going to do.

I had come from a family consisting of a brother, a great-aunt and my parents. I was now living with an Irish-Catholic family consisting of three sisters, four brothers, a grandmother and grandfather, plus Paul's parents. What a loving, wonderful, sharing family it was, and one with very strict moral and religious codes.

Before I moved into his home Paul and I had always gone out with a group. We hadn't paired off, but he had started picking me up after work and driving me home. I loved the beach and surfboard riding; he hated the beach. I loved roller skating; he loathed it. I liked dancing; he didn't. But we both loved the movies. I was wildly independent, and all of a sudden I had my own money. At home I had always given my wage packet to Mum, but now I had it to spend on myself. Paul saved his money; I didn't know the meaning of the word.

Needless to say, we fought constantly. But we had our good times, and he was wonderful to me. Despite our great friendship, though, I still couldn't or wouldn't open up, even to him, about my spirit friends and the voices.

My spirit friend Mary did not come with me when I left home. I knew this was the way it had to be, but the understanding did not help the loss I felt. My loss was twofold: Mary and Michael. We were now going our separate ways, and it took a long time for Michael to forgive me for leaving home. He had never really liked Dad, but he got on very well with our stepfather. I, on the other hand, understood a great deal about Dad and his drinking problem. I could forgive him easily.

Meanwhile, my relationship with Paul was becoming increasingly turbulent. I had grown very fond of his family and we shared that bond for many years, but it was no fun arguing with him all the time. Mum tried to get me back home, but that part of my life was over and, for a while, Mum and I didn't even talk to each other. I can see now how necessary this was for both of us. Through the experience of living with a 'normal' family I began to realise just how much responsibility I had always had.

Finally, the inevitable happened and I moved to a house my great-aunt owned. Because she lived permanently with my mum, my great-aunt had a housekeeper, Mrs Berry, living in the house and looking after it for her. I slept in my great-aunt's old bedroom. It was very big, with double French doors leading onto an upstairs balcony. There was a four-poster bed with mother-of-pearl inlay and a feather mattress – even a big mosquito net. Walking into that room was like walking into another era and, indeed, the whole house was like that, with old furniture that had been there for many years.

My great-uncle had died 30 years earlier. He had been a seaman and the things he had collected during his years at sea were to be seen all over the house. I still have his pipes and other treasures. It was wonderful touching things that had come from distant places and 'seeing' the pictures that emanated from them. Of course, I was practising psychometry, which is the name given to this ability, although I didn't know that then. I was only doing what I had always done, but this was my first opportunity to experience it with such unusual objects. This ability caused me many problems because I could not bear to part with any object I had tuned in to, and so my collection grew every time I moved. Thank God I eventually passed through this stage.

Neither the suburb nor the house I moved into were new to me. My dad's mother lived around the corner and quite a few of Dad's relatives lived nearby. Dad himself lived just down the road and would call in to check on how I was. Sometimes we would have a meal together. We always got on well when he wasn't drinking. There was no question where my loyalties lay – with my mum – but my sympathies were with Dad.

He was always loving, kind and thoughtful to me, and this became a very special time for the two of us, a time when our relationship deepened and a mutual understanding grew up between us. I'm grateful for that period in my life. I was eighteen years old and, aside from Dad's mother, Nanna Liz, he was the only person who could see what I saw and share an experience with me.

As time went by it became clear to me that someone else inhabited this house, someone other than those living. My bedroom was at the top of the stairs. On the landing before you reached my room was another bedroom, and on the landing before that was Mrs Berry's room. Every night, at the same time, footsteps could be heard walking up the stairs. They would stop on the second landing – the one before my room – and then the door would open and close.

At first I thought it was Mrs Berry. Then one day I asked her why she did this at exactly the same time each night, and why I didn't hear her bang the door again when she came back out.

'The house is haunted,' was her reply.

'Haunted?' I was imagining ghosts with two heads and all the usual things that this word conjured up.

Well, I locked my door that night, put the dressing table against it, added a few Hail Marys to the normal Lord's Prayer – and didn't sleep a wink. Next morning I was very sick.

At the age of thirteen I had developed a duodenal ulcer, which haemorrhaged from time to time. I know now that it was due to my highly emotional nature, coupled with the sensitive state I was in most of the time, and the constant battles at school with religion and trying to fit in. So, on this occasion, I wound up in hospital, having the usual injections and being kept under surveillance until I could go home. Dad came and collected me, and asked what I was upset about. When I finished telling him, he said, 'Well, didn't you ask who is haunting the place?'

'What do you mean, who?' I demanded. 'It's a ghost. Why should you want to know who it is?'

He persisted, and told me that if I asked, I would be pleasantly surprised.

That night Dad waited with me until eleven o'clock. We were sitting on the landing outside the haunted room when the heavy steps sounded on the staircase. I thought, 'How could you have believed it was tiny Mrs Berry, you dill.'

Suddenly, standing right in front of me was my great-uncle Mick, who had died a few years earlier. He had been the owner of Maggie, a dog I loved so much. I was so excited, and wanted to know what he was doing here and why he hadn't told me it was him. He said he had lived in this house many years before, and this had been his room. He told me he knew I was now living here and wanted me to know that I should never feel lonely. He would not come into my bedroom, and so had to wait until I was curious enough to come in search of him. He said he would stay in the house until I moved on.

When you experience this kind of contact with the spirit world, you learn many lessons that can go on unfolding for years. We can only comprehend a little more at each stage of our development. The main one for me at that time was learning that ghosts are not harmful as people believed, but merely people who have passed over. I was upset and angry that I had let my fear affect me so much that I suffered actual physical pain – and all because I had been carried away by Mrs Berry's fear, and had not reasoned it out myself. This was a hard lesson to learn, as were many more of the lessons still to come in my life.

I never did learn quickly. My problem was, and still is, that I expect people to understand what I am talking about. I expect them to use their commonsense. My troubles have never been with the other worlds or the people who inhabit them; they have always been with the people in this world who say that none of this exists because they can't see it and won't open their eyes.

It never occurred to me to ask my dad how he knew. By this stage of my life, he and I had shared experiences of seeing and talking to spirits. Years later I became aware that he, too, was learning and growing, but I still didn't ask him how he knew about the spirit world.

It didn't take me long to accept Mick's presence in the house, and his visits became a normal part of living there. Mrs Berry seemed to accept my explanation, but it was just not discussed. I did notice that she didn't go to bed as early as before, and only then realised that Mick had waited for her to retire before revealing himself through the eleven o'clock haunting episodes.

Six months later, a girlfriend whose family were having visitors from the country asked if she could stay the weekend with me.

We arranged for another girlfriend to stay as well, so that it would be easier for us all to leave early the next morning to go surfboard riding. So there we were, three girls in a big four-poster bed, which they found amusing and very old-fashioned.

'I thought you said there was only Mrs Berry in the house,' Lyn said.

'That's right.'

'I can hear a man's footsteps on the stairs,' she persisted.

'Oh, hell, Uncle Mick,' I said to myself. It hadn't entered my mind that this would happen – stupid me. I bluffed. 'It's your imagination,' I told her.

'Can you hear the footsteps?' Lyn asked Ann.

'Of course she can't,' I shouted, 'because you're imagining it.'

Well, by this time Ann wasn't sure what she could hear, thanks to all the commotion I was making. At that moment the door slammed. 'There you are,' I said, 'that's Mrs Berry going to bed.'

'I don't like this house,' said Lyn. 'It's spooky.'

Next day the boys picked us up. All was well, but I was nervous, afraid Lyn might say something. After lunch we were all sitting around, and what should she come out with but, 'Have you ever been to Margaret's house?'

'No,' they all replied.

I cut in, saying, 'It's not my fault – you know how strict Mrs Berry is.' Which is how I had always covered it before. And it was true to a degree.

Mrs Berry was like a silent sentinel, and the only boy allowed past the front gate was Paul. But even though she knew him, he had to sit in the kitchen to talk to me. We weren't allowed in the lounge room on our own. So I joked along with Lyn, Ann and the boys, thinking this would be the last time I would ever have anyone to stay. I just knew I was going to get the 'strange' treatment again.

That night, Lyn said, 'Let's stay downstairs and talk for a while before we go to bed.' The dining room was at the bottom of the stairs, so as we sat at the dining room table, the stairs were in plain sight. I tried to distract them by reminding them we were going board riding again early in the morning and should be in bed. They took no notice and kept talking: I have no idea what about because my mind was full of Uncle Mick. I reasoned that they wouldn't be able to see him, so all I had to do was bluff them about the footsteps.

Then the clock struck the hour and there he was. Nothing had prepared me for what happened next. Lyn saw him and Ann heard him, then Lyn went screaming out the front door with Ann not far behind. I chased them for two blocks, trying to reason with them – not an easy job under the circumstances! I have often looked back and thought how funny the scene must have looked to anyone in the street that night. Three girls, all in pyjamas, running and screaming at each other. And boy, did they run! I couldn't catch them.

I found out later that they didn't stop until they reached Lyn's house, where she collapsed into her mother's arms in a state of hysteria. One thing I learned that night: never assume anything, especially about other people seeing what I could see.

Next morning I told the boys we had had a fight and the girls had gone home. I didn't go to the beach that day because I had been ill all night, and anyway, I was panicking that the whole world would be talking about weird Margaret and the ghost. When the boys left my place to go to Lyn's, I was sure I would never go board riding with the group any more. They would just be laughing at me and making jokes. I wanted to sink into the earth and disappear forever.

Later the same day, Lyn's brother called in and asked me to go with him to his mother's house. 'Am I in trouble?' I asked.

'No,' he replied, 'Mum just wants to talk to you.'

I think that walk was one of the longest I have ever taken, like going to the electric chair, but Lyn's mother was great. We talked for hours, and this was the first time in my life that I was to hear the word 'medium'. Of course, I didn't know at the time that medium was what I would be called for the rest of my life.

Lyn was apprehensive with me, but she sat and listened to us talking and promised her mother she wouldn't spread the story

around. That afternoon Lyn walked me home and on the way
told me that Ann had left to go to her own house early that
morning. Mrs Page, Lyn's mother, had not been able to reason
with her, but Lyn was sure Ann would be alright when we got
together again.

We never did. Ann avoided me like the plague, and the story
of the haunted house became a local joke.

The effect of that incident was very different to what I had
been fearing. I was about to experience a whole new range of
horrors, things for which my limited knowledge of life, people
and the psychic world had not prepared me.

Mrs Page was a woman who had visited mediums for many
years to have readings done. She wasn't interested in the edu-
cational side, only in the psychic area which could tell her what
was happening in her life and what she could expect in the
future. She was completely unaware of the deeper, spiritual
aspects of mediumship.

At the time, of course, I thought I had found a miracle in Mrs
Page and her ideas of the spirit world. It was only months later
that I could be objective and realise that she saw nothing herself.
She was talking about other people's experiences and thoughts
and what she had read from books, while I thought we were
similar in so many ways.

I was welcome in her house. She would invite me for dinner
and I would go there from work, thinking what wonderful,
friendly people they were. I couldn't understand why I was so
tired all the time and why my sleep was fitful and plagued with
nightmares. I was suffering a lot of pain from my ulcer and, far
too often, being given injections for the pain. I could only eat
grilled food and never drank coffee or tea. From the day my
ulcer was diagnosed, I had been on a strict diet and learned the
hard way that any deviation from it caused severe pain. I had
been in hospital once when it haemorrhaged, so now I had learnt
to live with this ulcer and pamper it.

I couldn't understand why I was now feeling sick, and there
was no one around with enough knowledge of the psychic world
to explain what was happening. My guides no longer had

uninterrupted communication with me – all I knew was that I didn't have the same contact with them as I was used to having. Instead, I was receiving very accurate information from the spirit world about Mrs Page's life and her problems.

Giving her answers was just like second nature to me. She would ask me questions about the outcome of something, and it was as if I had discovered some sleeping facet of my personality whereby I could see events and happenings in a person's past and future. It was not long before Lyn was using me in the same way, and I was starting to enjoy these new discoveries about myself. Then Mrs Page began inviting friends around to have readings done, and I liked the novelty of the situation.

I had no idea at that stage that it was taking over my entire life. I was going to Mrs Page's house three or four times a week, and each session would last until quite late at night. The voice of reason would try to get a message through, but I would think to myself, 'How selfish you have become. These people need your help.' Increasingly I was hearing comments such as, 'Margaret, you look so tired,' 'You must be working too hard,' 'You'll have to rest more.' Of course, they meant rest from the job that was paying for my living, not my unpaid night-time work with them.

Finally, I collapsed at work and was admitted to hospital. The doctor said I was not looking after myself, and Mum pleaded with me to go home with her so she could take care of me. But I was stubborn, and still angry with her. Besides, being in the constant strained environment of the family home would make me sick anyway. I didn't say this to Mum; I just said, 'No.'

In those days, hospital visiting hours were limited and very strict, but that made no difference to my brother Michael. He would leave for school each morning and end up at the hospital instead, to sit with me. He would disappear when the doctors were doing their rounds, but never failed to reappear. Mum found out after a while, but she was powerless to change the situation. Punishment, threats, even dropping him at school on her way to work did no good. He would just turn up later and sit there looking at me.

We would talk some of the time, about anything and everything, but never about my anxieties. He wanted me to come home, yet never forced the issue. Neither of us realised it at the time, but what he was doing was giving me healing, a major role he was to play in my life. We understood this in later years, but then all I knew was that when he was there, I felt a sense of peace.

When I was discharged from hospital, Dad took me home and insisted on overseeing my medication and food intake. I had always suffered from motion sickness, and if I ate before travelling I just brought it up, so I had been in the habit of eating nothing until morning tea time. This meant I was getting no lining on my stomach and was always feeling sick when it came time to eat.

Determined to make my life easier, Dad and I started experimenting. He suggested plain biscuits, so I would try to eat one each morning after I got dressed. Most of the time I could only keep down a few bites, but when I got to work I would eat a whole one and it did help me until morning tea time. I couldn't digest milk and never drank it. I still can't, but at least I can manage a little in my coffee. Mrs Berry began giving me egg flips, and we discovered that if the milk was heavily flavoured, I could keep it down. It looked as though my physical self was on the mend.

Mrs Page started to call around again, appearing to be very concerned about me. After all the right words of concern, she would inevitably ask my advice about some problem, and that feeling of depression would come over me again. I would become confused and my nerves jagged, and it was obvious I was going through the same thing that had sent me to hospital, the only difference being that now I was doing all the right things physically. Dad said my depression was because I was worrying too much about other people's problems and literally suffering along with them.

In the end we decided I should stop giving readings, not because either of us realised exactly why I was getting ill, but because we knew I went downhill whenever I started trying to help people.

My biggest disappointment came when I tried to explain this to Mrs Page. I thought she and her daughter genuinely liked me, but they both stopped calling around. Hurt and confused, I finally had to face the fact that they were only interested in me if I was on tap for their readings. Sadly, this is something that still happens from time to time.

⟨⟩

I began to realise that when I opened myself up to my psychic side I was constantly being troubled by lost souls – people who had passed over in death and were lost in the lower astral dimension. At that time I didn't know the name of this place. I only knew that my rest was regularly being interrupted by spirits asking me for help of one kind or another – and it was not confined to night-times. It was upsetting me at all hours of the day and night, but of course I didn't try to explain this to anyone, which was why the medical profession blamed my nerves and my diet for my latest bout of ill health.

I talked to Dad, realising that I was feeling riddled with guilt at not knowing how to help these lost souls.

'What do they ask you to do for them?' Dad asked.

'In most cases they want me to let their relatives know they are alright.'

'Why don't you do it, then?' he wanted to know.

'How in the hell do I know who their relatives are and how to contact them? They'd think I was some kind of imbecile, anyway.'

'First things first,' said my dad.

One and then two nights a week Dad and I started sitting together at the table with a street directory and a phone book. I would give him the name of the spirit entity speaking to me and the suburb where he or she had lived. Dad would check the directory to make sure the street and suburb existed, then look in the phone book for a name that corresponded with the one I had been given. If he found one I would then ask who I was supposed to contact, and what I should say. Dad would write the information down so that we could go over it together later.

This was a very sad and difficult time, firstly because the spirits who spoke to me were people who had died under tragic circumstances, and I nearly always felt the pain they had suffered at the time of death. Secondly, we could not always check the information, since some of them had lived and died outside the area.

We discovered that the messages they wanted passed on to their loved ones were very personal. How does one write a letter to a bereaved person telling them that you have just been talking to their son or husband or whatever, and then proceed to give them the message? And this was just one of the problems we had to face at the time.

The worst feature of the whole business was that I had opened a floodgate, but instead of water pouring out, it was thousands of souls in distress, crying for help. I had no idea how to stop it. We did post some letters – we really had no choice – but I didn't give them my name or address. I thought my obligation was simply to pass on the messages without any further involvement on my part. You see, I was also very aware of the religious implications and didn't want people to persecute me. The memories of Mrs Page were still painful and I didn't want any more of the same trouble.

Nevertheless, what came out of these experiences formed the foundation that I would build on in the future when rescue work became an important part of my mediumship.

I had reached a stage where I found I was picking up people's thoughts as clearly as if they were speaking to me directly, and this was the beginning of another nightmare. It happened wherever there were people, which of course was everywhere. I hated getting on a bus or train, and couldn't stand being in a crowd because of the unbelievable bombardment of words.

Dad had started drinking far too much again, and I couldn't communicate with him. It was obvious he had his own problems and was also under psychic attack, with his only escape being alcohol. I couldn't talk about these experiences to Paul, who I'd started seeing again, and my grandmother was too old and sick. So there was no one. And because I didn't have a car, I couldn't avoid public transport.

I had grown accustomed to feeling the energy around individuals – in fact, it is something I have experienced all my life – but now I could feel other people's fear or sadness. My emotional nature was such that if a person was in a negative mood, that negativity would be the stronger energy and affect my attitude, too. If the person was happy, then that was a wonderful release for me, and I would often strike up a conversation with them to take my mind off the sad or angry vibrations around me.

This new development was totally different from what I had experienced before – it was a telepathic connection. My only previous telepathic experiences had been with the spirit world, and clearly, because of my readings, I had opened up another facet of my psychic nature.

At this time I hated going to work. I felt angry most of the time, and wasn't too happy with life in general. The moment I got on a bus the babble would hit me like a tidal wave, and whoever was angriest in the crowd would seem to be attacking me. Try to imagine your mind full of twenty or thirty people's thoughts, the arguments they had had before leaving home (or even the night before), resentment and anger against boss, wife, husband, child or in-law. I had no idea how to protect myself from all this, and kept hearing entire conversations that were going on in people's heads.

As with everything in life, there were lessons to be learnt from all of this. One was to be invaluable later when I was working with crowds of people while doing public demonstrations: I learnt to distinguish between spirit communication and telepathic connections, or extrasensory perceptions. I couldn't put a name to these things then; I just knew that people's thoughts, powerful as they might be, were not the same as the communications I had with the spirit world.

This enabled me to distinguish, while doing readings, those strong-minded people who were 'willing' me to tell them what they wanted to hear. For example, 'Will I marry this person I am involved with?' They want me to answer 'Yes,' when the right answer is 'No.' I call it self-fulfilling prophecy, when a person's will is so strong that they actually make something happen. In such cases, they would be far better off waiting for the right time – and that means in God's time.

I later did a lot of experiments with telepathic communication, and took on the role of sender as well as receiver, which taught me how powerful our thoughts can be and how we can influence others in a positive or negative way. The fact that I could send as well as receive influenced my whole approach to professional readings. I would deliberately avoid particular subjects when I knew the news was not good.

During these early days, when I was still having problems with unwanted telepathic communications, my work as a cashier in a city store caused me a lot of anguish. I had always loved working with the public and nothing had ever been too much trouble, but now I found everything an effort. I would be talking to a customer and at the same time hearing their innermost thoughts. Most of the time it was impossible for me to tell whether a person was reacting to me or to someone else altogether. I was taking it all personally, and the confusion was almost unbearable.

It's difficult to explain, but I was always arguing with myself, telling myself that Mrs Smith or someone didn't like me or they wouldn't be thinking such things about me. Then I would take the other side and argue that she couldn't be thinking these thoughts about me because she didn't even know me.

Things reached a point where I just had to do something. I had advanced to being a relief manager in the company where I had worked since I was fourteen and this involved quite a lot of travelling to other branches when a manager was sick or on leave. I was being very well paid, but now I felt I had to leave. (I was to return to that same company three times later on.) I found a job closer to home and with less responsibility.

My social life was just as devastating. I couldn't enjoy parties or going out with groups of people any more, although it was actually a party that changed everything for me.

Paul was insisting I go to a friend's twenty-first. I knew that some of his friends had not been happy with me for a while because of my problems and because they never knew how long our relationship would last this time. Still, they were Paul's friends, so I agreed to go.

The party was well under way when we arrived. (You should experience people's thought patterns when they have alcohol in their systems. They say people become less inhibited after a few drinks, and I know for a fact that their thoughts certainly do.) I was already wondering how long we would have to stay when my mind was assaulted by one of his friends thinking, 'How long is Margaret going to stay with him this time?'

That was understandable, but certainly not acceptable when he was saying something totally different with his mouth. I hate hypocrisy, and even today I can't come to terms with those who say one thing and mean the opposite. Then we moved on to chat to a group. A boy named Eric joined us and said, 'Oh, Margaret, you haven't met my girlfriend – I'll just go and get her.' As he returned, I looked at his girl and thought, 'She looks nice, and how pretty her dress is.'

'This is Denise,' Eric announced.

'Hello, Denise,' I replied. 'I'm Margaret.'

She started saying all the normal things one does in that situation, but just as clearly as if she was speaking the words – and like someone hitting me with a whip – her thoughts cut across my mind. She was thinking how much she hated my dress, and how she couldn't stand me. You can understand how upset I was, especially since I had barely said 'Hello', and she had monopolised the rest of the conversation.

In that split second I'm afraid I lost my temper. I hit Denise across the face and stalked out, and I can only imagine the scene after I left. Paul followed me out and drove me home, but there was no way I could explain it to him. So we argued all the way and our relationship was off again.

Have you ever had a really bad experience which led you to hate the world and its unfairness, and then later you find you can only thank God it happened? This was one of those episodes, and I can thank a complete stranger named Denise for my coming to understand that every man and woman is my teacher.

I did a lot of soul-searching that week, knowing I could not go through life like this. I realised I could never mix with the people at the party again, and I agonised over what to say in my own defence. I knew Denise would be the innocent one who would quite truthfully be saying, 'But I didn't do or say anything!', and I would only look worse if I tried to explain.

I was also upset and angry because so much had changed in my life – my job, my friends, and now my relationship with Paul. This was when I began making discoveries about mind power and self-healing. I decided that my mind had to be strong enough to block out other people's thoughts, and that whatever it took to achieve this, I would do.

❧

Today we hear a lot about positive thinking and the power of the mind, but thirty-four years ago there was no information available, or at least none that I was aware of. That was probably because I couldn't imagine anyone else was going through what I was, and I hadn't thought to seek answers from books.

I started with exercises, blocking everything from my mind with a white light. I surrounded myself with this light whenever people were around. Then I began practising self-hypnosis. I would stand in front of the dressing table mirror and look into my own eyes while I gave myself orders about my mind and what I wanted to achieve.

This was a strange period, and one which nearly ended my life a little later on. Meanwhile, I went on looking into the mirror, which I was using as a point of concentration, and inducing a relaxed state (similar to that used in meditation). But as soon as I reached that state, I would see different faces appearing in the mirror.

This was frightening at first, but I was only seeing what I had become used to from the spirit world. It was many years before I understood that, because of the relaxation, I was becoming 'intuned'. The thing that really bothered me, however, and made me cut down the time I spent in front of the mirror, was that my own face would distort and I would see someone else staring out at me.

I put up with this for as long as I could, but it unnerved me so much that I changed mirrors and just used a little one in which I could only see my eyes. It was years before I could once more stand and look at myself in a big mirror, so you can see what a big impact these experiences had on my mind.

Some people are born with the ability to go into this state of mind automatically. I didn't realise that I was one of these people. I never had to go through any process of relaxation to intune my subconscious and conscious mind. I was living in this reality every day.

Later on, I came to recognise those spirit faces I was seeing in the mirror, and who superimposed their faces over mine, as guides and teachers. I would see them regularly when sitting in my trance circle and during classes. This process, I was to learn, is called transfiguration. This is where the spirit guide can be seen using the medium's body to show the student what he looks like or what clothes he is wearing. Over the years my students saw and recognised my spirit guide Chang whenever we worked together.

What I was doing then was learning to close myself off from people's thoughts as soon as I realised they were intruding on my life again. In those days I used my mind for many experiments. I couldn't see any danger in what I was doing because it was working. I was feeling healthier and happier, and that was what mattered. Even when my ulcer began to play up again, I told myself I felt no pain.

⟡

When I was eighteen, I was approached to go back to work for my old company, with the added incentive of more money and a managerial position in my own shop. Of course, they thought I was twenty-one. I returned, and things were going well. I had not had problems with my ulcer for a long time – and then, unfortunately, I began bringing up blood. Once more I told myself I was alright and I felt no pain. I became sicker but would arrive at work each morning totally convinced that I was not ill and that my mind would fix this problem.

The staff told me I looked awful, the customers were asking what was wrong with me because of my dreadful grey colour, I was still bringing up blood, and I couldn't keep food down. After three weeks of this, I collapsed at work and was taken to hospital by ambulance.

As I was regaining consciousness I became aware of my surroundings. It was as though I was in a dream – there was a priest beside the bed, there were doctors, my mum and my brother. My arms were hooked to intravenous machines, and I knew I was having a blood transfusion, but it was all a wonderful feeling because I was in no pain and kept floating above my bed. I knew what everyone was saying, but there was this wonderful detached feeling.

I could see the familiar faces of my friends from the spirit world, and I was between the two worlds and everything was alright. I thought, 'What is the priest doing here?' and a spirit voice replied, 'He is giving you the last rites.'

'Good,' I thought, 'I hate this place anyway.' But then I looked at Mum, and it was as if I could see her life and my role in it right up to the end. Then I looked at Michael, and a most incredible sadness came over me. I could also see his future and my part in it. In that instant, I ceased feeling sorry for myself and shifted my consciousness from me to those I loved.

Intervention can come in many different ways, but at that time I was in that state between life and death where there is no pain or unhappiness. There was no peace of mind for me either, because I knew I couldn't leave the people I loved and have peace of mind on the other side, so it was better to stay and do what I could to help. This was no profound experience, but simply an understanding of what I had to do – and I did it. When I regained consciousness I asked my mum to send the priest away. She did, and she and Michael sat with me all night, quite unaware that they were giving me healing.

This was to be a quiet, self-induced period of isolation in my life. Despite having achieved some success with my techniques for protecting myself, I could not entirely close out all the intrusions by those unwanted spirit entities. I just had to learn to live with it. When I was approached by a spirit who had recently passed over and was lost or in trouble, I would talk to him or her exactly as I would speak to anyone in this world. Confronted with a problem that was outside my capacity to help, I would pray and ask God for assistance.

It was not unusual for spirits to return and thank me for helping. This was rewarding, and I learnt a lot about human nature in this way. I would ask them about life 'over there' and quickly understood that it was different things to different people. However, I also learnt that I couldn't take everything I was told at face value, because people interpret through their own filtering systems.

I encountered many spirits who believed, because of religious training and beliefs acquired here on earth, that they deserved their suffering. The stories of their lives would fill a book on its own. I discovered that the God of love, the one I firmly believed in, was not the same God that these troubled people knew. Theirs was a jealous God, a God of retribution, and I found myself having the same old arguments I had had at school. Some listened to my point of view, but some said I was working for the Devil.

Then a wonderful thing began to happen. A lot of spirits who had listened to me came back in groups, and they would talk to the distressed souls. When these people returned they were suffused with a clear white light, while the other poor souls were surrounded by grey or even black.

I was learning that my teachers didn't come from the same world I had been dealing with since I first began opening myself up spiritually. They came from a different dimension, one full of light, beauty and happiness, a world without pain. Now, at last, I was receiving messages from my long-lost teachers. I was overjoyed.

Through their teachings, I was beginning to understand a little about the emotional nature of human beings, the physical impact it can have, and how we can talk ourselves into ill health. This explained how misunderstandings and just plain ignorance had affected my life so much. My guiding spirits also told me that it was becoming increasingly difficult to get through to me because I was emitting so many negative thoughts that interfered with their communication. And all this was further complicated by the pain I was suffering, and the constant presence of unhappy spirits around me.

When I was very young, I had been able to pass through the lower astral with no difficulty, thanks to the protection of my guides and my own lack of fear. This had shielded me from attracting any of the wrong types. When I started to discover aspects of the lower astral, my guides didn't interfere because they knew I was learning valuable lessons. And now, I was learning how to protect myself from troubled souls, and communicate more clearly with those who had moved into the light of a higher dimension.

About this time, I moved out of my great-aunt's house and into another suburb. My stepfather and my mum, who was now pregnant with my sister, moved into my great-aunt's house. They lived there for twelve months, then moved a fair distance away. Our relationship had not really improved and I didn't see much of Mum, although she did come to visit me every so often.

Dad had moved into the house where I was living and everything was going well between us. I started dating Paul again and we became engaged. This time I was determined to make it work. I had kept up my relationship with his family and they had always gone out of their way for me. This stayed the same for many years, even though the planned marriage never did take place.

I decided on a complete job change. I reasoned that if I could understand why people drank alcohol and what made them do it, I might be able to help Dad.

When I told Paul, a non-drinker, that I wanted to work in a hotel, he burst out laughing. 'You must be joking,' he said.

I was very indignant. 'I am nineteen,' I replied, 'and quite old enough to do what I want.' He stopped laughing when he saw I was serious. He told me I would lose my temper as soon as someone swore at me or said a word out of place and, when this didn't work, he said people would think I was cheap, working in a hotel. When this had no effect either, he drove me to his house so his parents could talk me out of it. They couldn't.

Later the same week, the family came up with an idea based on the belief that I would not last a week behind a bar. Through various family connections, they organised an interview for me at a hotel where they knew the manager. If I was going to work in a hotel, it might as well be where someone could keep an eye on me.

I started work the following week and stayed there for three years. It was a family hotel, no one ever swore at me and I made friends with many people, including Patricia Cashman. Pat taught me bar work, and remains a loving and generous friend.

My relationship with my mum was re-established by now, but because she lived so far away, we communicated mainly by phone.

I had retained one friend from the incident at the party with Paul – a girl named Janis. Although we had not seen much of each other for two years, Janis and I were still good friends. She was ten years older than me, and she was now married to a friend of Paul's whose surname was Dent. The four of us often went out together.

To this day I don't know why, but for some time I had joked with Janis about how one day she and I would be sisters and have the same surname. She and I used to puzzle over this, and we even thought it might be some sort of carry-over from a previous life. Janis was more aware than anyone else of the complexities of my relationship with Paul. She was one of the few people – in fact, the only one until I met Pat – with whom I could be completely honest.

Anyway, a young man came into the hotel one day and we started talking. He was from out of town and had recently moved to the city with his aunt, uncle and young cousin. He was very involved with roller skating and I was still an ardent roller skater. Along with my board riding, skating was still one of the bones of contention between Paul and me, but there was no way he could make me give up my favourite pastimes.

The young man was called Bob, and when he asked me to go out with him, I said, 'Yes.' We arranged to meet later the same week to go to a drive-in movie, and I asked him to meet me at the local Town Hall so Dad and Paul wouldn't find out. I had never done anything like that before. I talked to Janis, and we decided that if I could live with this betrayal, then good luck to me.

I went to the drive-in with Bob, but had a miserable time because I felt so guilty. I was such bad company I felt sure Bob wouldn't ask me out again.

Meanwhile, I was increasingly unhappy about my coming marriage to Paul. I confided in Pat and she helped me a lot. She made me realise it wasn't my fault that Paul and I couldn't communicate or enjoy the same things – or, for that matter, even *want* the same things out of life. I had always felt guilty at not being the person he wanted me to be, but it was one thing to feel like that and another to know what to do about it.

The day after my talk with Pat, I told Paul I was not ready to get married. This time we both knew it was really over. We remained good friends, and became even better friends once we were both married to other people. I suppose that was because we were at last growing up.

I started dating Bob. One day Janis asked me, 'What's his surname?'

Would you believe, I didn't know? I had been introduced to him by his first name and had never thought to ask his surname. 'I'll find out tonight when I see him,' I told Janis. I did, and the moment I arrived home, I rang her. It was late and she was in bed.

'Guess what his surname is?' I asked.

'How would I know?' she replied testily.

When I told her, she immediately forgave me for ringing her so late. His name was Dent, the same as hers. I married Bob when I was twenty-two years old, sharing Janis's surname as we had joked I would all that time ago. Bob and I have already celebrated our thirtieth wedding anniversary, so the name Dent has now been with me for more than half my life.

With all this going on in my personal life, I hadn't seen Dad's mother for some weeks. At work one day I became very depressed. A feeling of gloom swamped me. I found myself preoccupied with thoughts of my Nanna Liz, and felt guilty that I hadn't called in to see her. Our relationship was especially close, as she no longer saw Michael because of the rifts in our family. That day, my mind was so full of Nanna that I decided to leave work early to visit her.

I rang a friend, Sue, who picked me up and drove me to my grandmother's house, which was a two-storey semi-detached with a park along one side. Nanna was bedridden at this stage and so we would stand down below and yell at her to throw down the front door key. But when we pulled up outside her house this day, the most powerful feeling of loss overwhelmed me. I said to Sue, 'She's not here, she's in hospital.'

'Call out and check,' she suggested.

I got out of the car, knowing it was useless. When I called out, a neighbour came out and said, 'They took her to hospital this morning.'

'What time?'

'Ten o'clock.'

I knew that, because it was the same time I had started thinking about her.

We drove off, heading for the hospital, but we had only driven a couple of blocks when I burst into tears. 'She's dead,' I said. 'What's the time?'

Sue told me, and we arrived at the hospital ten minutes later. As we got out of the car I said, 'It's no good, it's all over,' but we continued towards the entrance and reached it just as my cousin was coming out. He looked at me and I said, 'She's gone, hasn't she?'

'Yes,' he said, 'we've been trying to contact you all day.'

I was riddled with guilt. I hated myself for not having seen her before she went, and for not having been there when she died. As for being any help to my dad in his grief, I was too sorry for myself to think about that.

I had already learnt to check my facts. This is something I teach to all my development classes. You have to be able to distinguish between your imagination, psychic impression and spirit communication. So, when something happens, you note the exact times, and later you will find that they correspond. My nanna had died at exactly the time I said she had.

Her funeral was the most beautiful experience I have ever known and it was Nanna Liz herself, at her own funeral, who made me come to terms with her death. The service was held in the local Catholic church. She was in an open coffin and the church was packed. I walked up the aisle, dreading going to the coffin because I was afraid. I was thinking, 'How angry she must be with me. She probably doesn't even want me at her funeral.' I kissed the lifeless form and at once knew she was not in her body. I sat down, the church service began, and I found myself crying.

Then, without warning, the entire atmosphere of the church suddenly changed for me. It became alive with light, and my grandmother was standing in the aisle as plainly as any live person there. Her first words were, 'Don't be a hypocrite. Why are you crying? It's not for me – you're crying for yourself.'

I was shocked at this. Here we were in church, people sobbing and being very solemn while Nanna Liz was busy walking up and down the aisle giving me the benefit of what she really felt, good and bad, about the different members of the family who had gathered to see her off.

When she finally stopped speaking, I continued to answer her with my mind and said how sorry I was that I hadn't seen her before she died. I burst into tears and someone's arm went round my shoulder, but now my tears were tears of joy. I felt so happy for Nanna, knowing it was such a wonderful release. She told me not to go to the burial as she would not be there. It transpired she had only come to the church to see her funeral and then would go on to her heaven.

I couldn't get out of the church fast enough to find Dad and tell him that Nanna had been in the church talking to me. 'I know,' he said. 'Let's go home.' And we walked out of the churchyard together without looking back. I have communicated with Nanna many times since her passing. She is a much loved friend, and we enjoy a relationship that was never possible when she was alive.

A whole new chapter was starting for me. I was leaving a lot of people behind. Dad moved on, Mum had a baby girl, Michael started work and I was involved with someone I loved. I was determined not to make the same mistakes with Bob that I had with Paul.

After we had been seeing each other for some months, I decided I had to tell him about the other side of my nature. I was older now, more experienced in psychic matters, and understood much more about myself than I had when I was fourteen and first becoming involved with Paul. I knew that by telling Bob I risked losing him, but I also knew that if we were to have a future together, I couldn't go through life hiding things from him.

I still had not entirely got on top of my ulcer, but I was better than I had been for many years. I was using a self-healing process and trying to stay calm emotionally, so it was under control. Janis, too, had suffered from an ulcer for many years before I developed mine, so we were kindred spirits. We shared a sort of tranquil energy and mutual understanding that helped us in many ways we could not have found with anyone else.

I finally summoned up enough courage to talk to Bob about psychic phenomena and the little I knew about them. Poor Bob! I have often asked him since if he would have run a mile had he known what lay in front of him by marrying me. Of course, he always says he wouldn't change anything, and I choose to believe him. I do believe his life would not have been as interesting without me and the thousands of people – dead and alive – who come and go in our lives.

3

*M*Y EARLY LIFE WITH BOB

I WAS ASLEEP AND DREAMING. A man dressed in the full regalia of a Catholic bishop, including the ceremonial cap, came to me and told me I must visit a spiritualist church in a neighbouring suburb.

'But that's witchcraft,' I replied, alarmed.

'No, it is not – and don't be afraid. Telephone the church. An old lady will answer and tell you what to do.'

I woke up at once. I was distressed and couldn't go back to sleep. Who was this man, anyway? Probably some religious fanatic, or worse still, someone involved with dark works. I had no idea what dark works or witchcraft consisted of at that time, but I had heard enough to know that evil existed.

In the morning I was too upset to go to work, so I rang Mum, who arrived a couple of hours later. When I told her about the bishop, Mum said, 'Remember Mrs Johnson, the lady who gave me a reading when I was fifteen? She was a spiritualist and well known for her good work. Let's look in the phone book to see if there really is such a church.'

We looked, and there it was.

'You ring,' I said.

'No,' said Mum. 'What good will that do? You have to speak to the lady, but I'll stand next to you in the phone box and come with you to the church.'

I felt afraid, but I reasoned that it was only a phone call and I could always hang up. Imagine the shock when I phoned and the voice on the other end was indeed that of an old lady. I didn't know what else to do, so I told her the truth.

'Yes,' she said, 'I know. I've been expecting you to call.'

I went cold. Mum was standing so close to me that she could hear, and we just looked at each other in astonishment. Then the voice told me to come along on a particular night and I would meet some people who could help me.

Mum came with me that night. The address was an old house that had been converted into a church. We had to ring the front doorbell to get in because it was not a church service evening. Inside there were theatre seats and a platform, a piano, and some pictures of Jesus on the walls, but on this night only a few people were there sitting in the kitchen, having come for development and healing.

I must say that, at my age, it seemed very spooky and I was suspicious and unsettled. I hadn't come in contact with people like this before. They all looked very normal, although they seemed quite ancient to me. The lady I had talked to on the phone was Alice Scott. There was also a man named Clarrie Floyd, and several others. They were people who held down ordinary jobs but were forced to lead double lives. Some were housewives who had to lie to their husbands about where they were going and what they were doing. Many raised families who never knew about their healing or mediumship abilities.

Clarrie was to become my mentor and teacher, as well as a much cherished friend until he died six years later. Through him and others in the group, I learned to understand much more about my psychic abilities and how to use them to help others. I also learned that I was not one of a kind, and that was a great revelation. But that first night, I had no idea I was starting on a path that would bring me tremendous joy and love, a deeper understanding of the meaning of God, untold changes in my life, and contact with thousands of people – as well as the incredible loneliness that comes with the gift of mediumship.

I attended the closed circle one night a week. We sat around the kitchen table and started the meetings with a prayer. Clarrie would go into a trance and his guide, Roy, would come through and answer questions about his world; whenever we asked, he would give advice on how to help some person we were praying for. Roy had lived on an island when he was incarnated in our world and had died, as a young man, in a drowning accident. He was a black man with wiry black hair, and he never wore shoes. He had been with Clarrie since Clarrie was a small boy.

Clarrie's life had been one continual struggle. From the day he was old enough to speak, he had been unable to utter a word without stuttering, and it was only through the perseverance and faith of his mother that he had learnt to talk at all. He had also spent his life in callipers, and wore thick, heavy boots. You always knew when Clarrie was coming; you could hear his heavy steps and the scraping sound he made when he limped. He lived in a one-bedroom flat, was on a pension, and travelled by public transport.

He did a lot of work as a platform medium, and went wherever he was needed, which sometimes involved long train journeys because there were never enough mediums to do all the work. They were always overworked, and received no pay for their gifts. I don't know one of them who didn't live and die in poverty, yet to see these people was a gift in itself. Their indisputable survival evidence left no doubt that there is life after death.

Meanwhile, I was still working in the hotel and spending a lot of time with Bob. The job hadn't given me any greater understanding of why people drink to excess – in fact I was even more confused; but it was helping me in many other ways. I was growing more confident, and I was understanding more about my psychic experiences.

After Bob and I married in 1968, we moved into a one-bedroom flat. In the bedroom, we had a double bed, a dressing table and a wardrobe. It was a lovely big room with plenty of space between the foot of the bed and the dressing table. Bob left for work at 6 am and I left at 8.30 am. Every morning as I was making the bed I would notice it had moved away from the window, so I would push it back. This was difficult because it was so heavy. I would leave for work thinking how odd this was, because each morning it seemed to be a little further out than last time.

One evening I was having a chat with Clarrie before our circle, and he said, 'What problems are you having with your bed, Margaret?'

I was surprised he knew, but told him the story.

'Well,' he said, 'I have a message for you. I am being told that a spirit guide is doing this so he can give proof of his existence to Bob.'

'Bob doesn't need proof,' I said, 'and when he goes to sleep, an earthquake wouldn't wake him. Anyway, I'm the one who has to make the bed, so all it's doing is making more work for me.'

Clarrie persisted, saying, 'I'm sure Bob isn't telling you all that's going on.'

Despite Clarrie's comments, I decided not to say anything to Bob; I would just leave well enough alone and keep putting the bed back. About a week later, however, I was woken from a sound sleep at four in the morning by Bob. He was shaking me and screaming something. He jumped out of bed and put the light on, obviously very disturbed. 'Get him out, get him out!' he kept shouting.

'Who?'

He pointed to the back of the bed. I turned and saw, as clearly as if he had been flesh and blood, a tall, strong black man. I leapt out of bed and found the bed was so far into the middle of the room that I couldn't stand between it and the dressing table. I stood transfixed while this man just looked at us. He had a wide, friendly smile on his face, and his size ceased to frighten me.

'I'm going to make a cup of coffee,' Bob said, starting for the kitchen.

'Wait,' I called, 'don't you want to hear what he has to say?'

'You can tell me what he says. Just get him out of my bedroom.'

'My hero,' I thought. I had no choice but to talk to this big black man myself.

He told me he was Bob's guide and had not wanted to frighten him. For some time he had been doing things to get Bob's attention, one of which was moving the bed. He told me some details about himself, and said the problem was that every time he tried catching Bob's attention, Bob's easy-going nature would just put it down to a natural occurrence. He was running out of patience because his messages weren't being heeded.

I went out to the kitchen and told Bob what he had said. I was quite amazed by his reply. It was to give me an insight into this man I had married, and his wonderful attitude to the spirit world.

'I know someone has been moving the bed,' he told me. 'I find it there every morning, but you are still asleep. I realise someone has been playing tricks on me; I know there are spirits, and I know there is a life after death — so why did he have to wake me up and give me the biggest fright I have ever had in my life?'

'Because,' I said, 'he wanted you to acknowledge his presence so he could give you some spiritual direction and teachings. Anyway, why didn't you tell me all this?'

'Well, from now on I will,' he said, rather heatedly. 'I don't want that experience again.'

Bob was true to his word. That was the beginning of more than thirty years of him telling me every tiny detail about messages and spiritual experiences, at any hour of the day or night. Bob's most relaxed state is when he is going to sleep, so it is easy for the teachers and guides from the spirit world to communicate with him then. Often, I would be drifting off to sleep and Bob would wake me up to relay what he was being taught.

This wasn't the last of Bob's early experiences. About a fortnight later I was in the lounge room watching television and Bob was in bed. I heard footsteps moving from the front door into our bedroom, and they were making the exact sounds that Clarrie made with his slow, heavy tread and one foot scraping.

I was confused, and thought, 'Is Clarrie alright?' I had seen him only that day, so he couldn't be dead. Then I heard Bob's agitated voice from the bedroom.

'Margaret, come here!'

I went in and Bob said, 'Will you please tell Roy to go back to Clarrie and let me get some sleep?' And there was Clarrie's guide, Roy, sitting on the side of our bed, talking to Bob.

I was still worried about Clarrie, but Roy assured me he was asleep in his bed. So why had we heard Clarrie's footsteps? Roy had a great sense of humour and would say things in such a matter-of-fact way that the impact was twice as funny. Straight-faced, he told us that we wouldn't have heard anything if he had walked in his bare feet, so he had decided to sound like Clarrie. He said we would always know when he was around in future because we would always hear him coming in the same way.

Bob can see spirits. Not all the time, and not always in the detail of the black man or Roy; but he can sense them and often sees the shape, so he can tell if it is man, woman, or child.

⁓

Life went on pretty much as normal, if you can call it normal to have the experiences I continued to have. But I was to come very close to death, and learn a lot as a result. One day I had a half day off work. A girl named Terry, who had recently started at work, asked if I would like a lift, since she also had the afternoon off. As we approached her car, a terrible feeling of gloom came over me. I told myself not to be stupid and shrugged it off.

We had gone about three blocks and I was still fighting with the worries in my mind. I told myself it was because Terry's car was a Mini Minor and I had never been in such a small car before. The next thing I knew, I was being hurtled through the air.

When I regained consciousness I was flat on my back and a policeman was looking down at me. He was holding my head in his arms. 'What happened?' I asked.

'A car came straight through the stop sign and hit yours, sending you flying out the door,' he told me. I tried to look around and could see I was on the footpath. Someone put a blanket over me.

'Did I get thrown all this way?' I wanted to know.

'Yes,' said the policeman. 'I was on my way home and saw what happened. Don't try to move.'

'Don't worry. I can't feel a thing.'

The next thing I remember is being examined at hospital and the doctor saying, 'I'm very sorry, Mrs Dent, but you've lost your baby.'

'What baby?'

'You were about three months pregnant.'

I hadn't known, and I suppose I was in shock. The same policeman came in and I asked if he would call my husband. 'I have,' he said. 'I got the information from the girl who was driving. She escaped serious injury somehow.'

I said, 'I've lost my baby. I'm badly bruised but nothing is broken. My back is the problem, but I don't want them admitting me to hospital. I don't want them to touch me. My husband will take me home and I will get all the healing I need.'

'Alright,' he agreed, and walked out the door.

Soon after, the doctor came and asked me to sign the release papers. He told me he thought I was being very foolish, and that he would have to talk to my husband when he arrived. The policeman returned, and I thanked him for talking to the doctor.

'Would it be too much trouble for you to tell my husband when he comes?' I pleaded. 'I want to see him before the doctor does.' I described Bob and what he would be wearing, and the policeman met him as he came into casualty. Bob came straight in to see me, and I explained why I didn't want to stay in hospital. He was very distressed, but he trusted my judgment and supported my decision when he talked to the doctor.

I never saw that policeman again after that day, but we shared something. He was only a couple of years older than me with dark hair and brown eyes, and he radiated an unusual compassion. I looked into his eyes and felt as if I was talking to a life-long friend.

I was in bed at home for quite some time. The family doctor took care of my medical requirements, and my friends in both worlds gave me healing. The bruises and gravel rash improved very quickly, since spiritual healing accelerates the body's natural healing processes. My back was the main problem. Clarrie told me if I put myself in the hands of the medical profession, they would want to operate. This confirmed what I had felt in hospital and, on three occasions over the next ten years, doctors wanted to operate on my back. Whenever it is particularly bad I have healing sessions, enabling me to go through life without constant pain.

During this period of enforced relaxation I was given a lot of direction from my guides. I was told I would have a baby boy, and that my education would take another direction for a while.

I duly conceived and had a very difficult pregnancy, going in and out of hospital several times. After my son, whom we named John, was born, I stayed on in hospital and my mum and Bob took him home to Mum's house. When I finally came home I had to stay in bed and couldn't do much at all. My back was starting to improve, but it was obvious something else was wrong with me. Despite being on the correct diet for a duodenal ulcer, I couldn't keep anything down, and I was in a lot of pain. But even though it was in the same area as an ulcer, the pain felt different. The doctors, however, kept treating me for an ulcer.

A lot of tests followed and the last ones revealed I had a gall-stone almost the size of my gall bladder. The doctors had thought I was too young to suffer from this problem, so left those tests until last. When it was diagnosed, they said it was consistent with a woman in her sixties, not someone my age.

I was too weak to be operated on. After John was born I had contracted pneumonia, and now I was sick with it for the third time, so the doctors were worried about the effect of an anaes-thetic. It was to be many months before they felt it was safe to operate, and I was very ill the whole time. When eventually they did operate, I found myself once more standing at the door between two worlds. They removed my gall bladder and I can remember watching my body after the operation. I was looking at myself in the hospital bed with Bob on one side, my mum on the other, and the hustle and bustle of the medical staff all around. I was aware of how worried they were, and I knew that Michael was outside. I also knew that I was not going to die and that I had no decision to make – my whole being was aware that I would recover, and that was that. I did, and the speed of my recovery amazed everyone. In only a matter of weeks I was ready to go back to work, even though I had contracted pneumonia again in hospital.

⊶⟡⊷

We moved suburbs, which brought us closer to where Mum lived. I had kept up my very close friendship with Clarrie, and stayed in touch with several other mediums. Bob and I were living in a first floor flat with two bedrooms and polished floors throughout.

Now I had to look for work. I could have gone back to my old job, but it was too far to travel, so I started a new job closer to home.

Bob and I would often sit together, and I would go into a meditative state and give messages and teachings from the other side. Whenever Clarrie came to dinner, a sitting always followed. This was the time in my life when I began to understand spiritual healing – as my guides had told me I would. I was still having health problems, although not as badly as in previous years. It was becoming clear that I was developing asthma, and my attitude to this was one of anger and refusal. No way was I going to have the same life as my mum had; I wasn't going to be classed as an asthmatic. I would fight it.

Looking back now, I can see what happened to me. Out of my anger came the need to educate myself. That meant learning to take control myself, instead of letting things control me. It was the old fate story all over again. Nothing is inevitable; we can alter the course of our lives. I was learning the lesson of responsibility. Previously, I had just accepted the ulcer, the back problems and the gallstone because I believed I had no say in the matter. I had thought faith was the only thing one needed as part of the healing process, and didn't realise that one can stop the progress of an illness by using self-healing. I had been one of those people who experience the symptoms of a complaint long before the illness itself develops.

In those days, if I had had the knowledge that I acquired over the years, I could have avoided quite a few health problems. I was young, however, and even when I did contact people who were working in this area, I found their knowledge was also limited. The attitude was that nothing could be done to prevent ill health, but spiritual healing could take away the pain and sometimes perhaps cure the complaint.

If you were cured it was karma, and the suffering was part of your spiritual growth. Very little, if anything, was said or known about the mind's power to cause health problems, and absolutely nothing was mentioned about the effect of spiritual work on one's health. It was recognised that all forms of mediumship drained physical energy, but this was supposed to be just part and parcel of the work. I do know that human beings learn from pain. I also accept that, for some people, this is the only way; but I don't believe it is necessary for all of us to learn in this manner.

I came to the understanding that the best teachers are those who teach from personal experience, and I must have driven the kind souls on the other side mad. I had always asked questions, but I had also accepted the answers that felt right to me. Now I had to know how everything worked and why.

My guides advised me strongly not to read books on the subject, whether about the spirit world, mediumship or healing. I was told: 'You have developed to a certain level through natural progression. Every proof you receive you accept without preconceived ideas, making it more evidential to you. It is better not to read of the experiences of others and how they interpret them. When you are strong in your gifts and balanced in your own interpretations, then read whatever you like.'

I am so grateful for the advice I was given in those early days. By not reading books, I could publicly and truthfully state that I teach what I have seen, what I remember and what I know to be true.

Bob, Clarrie and I would sit whenever we could, and we might be joined by Mum, or sometimes by my brother Michael. I would receive teachings and pass them on to the others. I was clearly going through changes in my mediumship. I was not yet at the stage where I could allow myself to be completely taken into trance; I didn't want to. I was happy with the way things were going but, like all things that grow, we evolve whether we like it or not.

One thing happening to me was that I was going through transfiguration. The faces of people in the spirit world would superimpose themselves on my face. This is what had happened before, when I was experimenting with hypnotherapy and using the mirrors. That had really frightened me. The difference now was that I couldn't see the changes, and Clarrie was with me, so I was not afraid. Mum had been very close to her grandfather, and when his face appeared it was wonderful for her. I didn't know the man then, but I was to have a lot to do with him in the future.

It was at this time in my life that Michael died. Although I realised quickly that he was still with me, and learnt much from him about the spirit world, it was a difficult period.

We decided to make a fresh start in another city, so Bob, John and I moved into Bob's mother's house with her. Ann, Michael's widow, had settled into her new flat and Mum was still with my stepfather. I was still grieving. I missed Michael and my sadness interfered with our communication. He had to adjust to his new world, and I had to adjust to a world without him while settling into a new life in a new city.

Through my work with grief, I have come to understand it and the stages that people go through. The difference with people like myself is that we can pass through these stages more quickly than those who don't know what has happened to their loved ones.

Grief becomes very different when a person thinks 'dead' means 'dead', that there is nothing beyond; but missing the physical presence of that loved one is the same for everyone. I had experienced the loss of my grandmother and my much loved great-aunt. I had lost my great-uncle, too, and would feel the loss of many others in the years ahead.

Michael has taught me so much about the spirit world. I have shared with him experiences that we never could have shared when he was alive and, wonderfully, have seen more of him than of any other person who has passed over. And yet, despite all this, he is still my saddest loss.

I tried to get on with my life. I went to work and John started school. My friends were very supportive, not letting distance stop them, and old friends came up for the weekend to spend time with us.

I was sad that Clarrie only came to visit once, but realised it was hard for him to sit for so long in the train. One day I was home alone watching television when something urged me to turn the television off. Suddenly, I was aware of quietness and stillness in the room. I knew this heralded something extraordinary, so I made myself comfortable, relaxed physically and mentally and, in a short time, my spirit left my body. The next thing I knew, I was in Clarrie's lounge room. He was sitting in his chair and he was dead.

'No,' I cried, 'don't leave me, not you too.'

Instantly I was back in my own home and Clarrie's spirit was there with me. All I could ask was 'Why?'

He told me he had had a choice: he could have lived another five years, but the deterioration of his body would have got worse and healing could only do so much. He had been in pain all his life and wanted no more.

I was angry. 'But there is so much work I want to do,' I said to him.

'I will always be with you,' he replied, 'and I can help you now more than ever before.'

I must have seemed like a spoilt child at the time. I was shocked and upset, and my arguments made no sense because he was already dead. Logic had no place in my thoughts, only emotions. Dear Clarrie had taken the time and a lot of effort to appear to me. He was making the transition to his new world and could stay no longer. Our communication was beginning to weaken, and we both knew it was time for him to leave.

I composed myself, then rang someone and asked them to go to his flat. When Bob came home I told him, and he rightly defended Clarrie's decision to go early, which helped. As soon as practical our mutual friends gathered and had a sitting. Clarrie and Roy communicated with us for hours, and we were all so happy for him at the end of the sitting that we could never again think of his passing with feelings of sorrow or anger.

Friends of relatives and just friends of friends began coming to me for guidance, but at this point I would go to their homes whenever possible. I didn't want a repetition of what had happened to me before. Many people told me I should give up my job and do readings for a living. My reply was always, 'No way.'

Michael and I were in constant contact. He was telling me about things he was experiencing in the spirit world and, whenever possible, I would travel on the astral with him.

One day Michael came to me and told me things weren't going well for Ann, and the baby was sick. I got home from work soon after to find Ann and the two boys waiting for me. They moved in with us, and Ann, Bob and I started a circle. We sat one night a week, which was the beginning of my trance mediumship.

I have conducted hundreds of circles since those early days, frequently involving trance work, yet those early sessions with just the three of us were so special that they can never be reproduced. I suppose it was the excitement of new discovery, learning what the spirit side of life can give us, and the amazing sensation of having someone else's personality come into my mind and body. There was endless joy in completely leaving my body, with spirit friends taking me to special places where I could talk, listen, observe and learn.

꧁꧂

In 1975 the time had come to move back south. This time we rented a house with three small bedrooms and I was able to use one of them for readings.

I made a friend, Carmel, who asked if I would do readings for three or four of her friends. I agreed, and wasn't worried because I had done the same sort of thing before. I would take a piece of jewellery from each person and give them the information I received. Because a reading is a very personal thing, a room was always allocated for my use, so I could talk privately to each individual. It was not unusual for me to spend two or three hours with one person, and my fee was two dollars.

When I arrived at Carmel's home, however, there were fifteen women there.

'This is impossible,' I told her.

She was as upset as I was, because each woman invited had brought relatives and friends with her. The session was to become my first public demonstration and, at that time, I thought it would be my last. I couldn't read for all these people in the way I had been doing, and to see them individually would take a week. I asked Carmel to collect a piece of jewellery from each woman and put them all into a bowl. I then took an item from the bowl without knowing whose it was, gave the messages I received, and asked if the owner had any questions.

I remember one of those readings very vividly, because it gave me so much pain and anguish. The last piece of jewellery in the bowl was a diamond ring, and I proceeded to treat it in the same way I had the others.

'There is a lady by the name of May in spirit,' I said, 'and she is on your mother's side of the family tree. With her is another lady named Sarah, and Jim is saying hello.' The owner of the ring spoke up before I had time to ask. She was very excited and said the names belonged to her mother, father and aunt, all of whom had passed over some time ago. I then gave her various messages from these people, proving to her that they were indeed the family members she thought they were.

All was going well and I was about to finish the reading when her father said, 'I want you to give her the following message: "Your sister Mary is with us".' I repeated his words aloud, and immediately the woman became very upset.

'That's wrong!' she said. 'My sister Mary lives in England and I was talking to her on the phone yesterday.'

I said this was the message I had been given, and she started to argue with me. I told her we should leave it at that and closed the reading. I was apprehensive, wondering what I had done wrong. Perhaps I had misunderstood the message. I couldn't change what I had said because that's what I had been told –

and yet I began to doubt both myself and my ability.

I decided I wasn't good enough to charge people for readings, that I'd get a 'real' job the next day. I had never felt so depressed and exhausted in my life. Of the fifteen people there that day only twelve could afford to pay, so what with the petrol and the money I had given Carmel for cakes and biscuits, I had made nothing out of the session anyway.

At eight o'clock that night the phone rang. It was Carmel, telling me that the woman with the sister in England had rung her that afternoon. It appeared that soon after arriving home from Carmel's house, she received a telegram asking her to phone England. When she phoned, she was told her sister Mary had died suddenly from a heart attack. She asked what time this had happened and, when she hung up, worked out that, allowing for the time difference, it was exactly when I had received the message from her father.

She then rang Carmel and asked her to let me know – but Carmel had been busy and didn't get around to it until about six hours later. This was my first experience of people being so insensitive to my sensitivity. It was, however, kind and thoughtful of the bereaved woman to send me the news in her time of grief. Later, I saw her privately and we had a number of sittings where I was able to bring her sister through. She is my client to this day, coming once a year over all these years. She has also become a student of mine and has developed her own mediumship capabilities, which she uses to help others.

Over the next few years our financial situation was always precarious and the twelve months immediately ahead of me were to be a nightmare of self-doubt and mental and physical exhaustion. At no time in my life, before or since, have I cried as many tears as I did that year. When Bob came home, we would talk over the day's events and he would make me feel better. I needed his faith and commonsense to remind me that I was doing a lot to help people; yet nothing could take away the dreadful feeling of responsibility the readings involved.

4

$\mathcal{P}$UTTING MY PSYCHIC ABILITIES TO WORK

I DO NOT CLAIM SUPERHUMAN POWERS, nor do I think I am some kind of angel. God has made me an instrument through which He works, by way of those people who live in the spirit world. These souls choose to teach and enlighten mankind, and I am simply the channel through which they communicate. On my own I can do nothing; but when I work with spirit, anything is possible. I have all the frailties of a human being, but my eternal searching and 'prove-it-to me' attitude has meant that I can stand up today, backed by the testimony of so many people, and say: 'Yes, I did this, but it is not really I who did it; it is God working through me.'

In 1976, about a year after my nerve-racking experience at Carmel's place, I gave my first public demonstration. I was so nervous, I couldn't eat or drink anything – and thirty years on I am still the same. The only way I can ever get up in front of a group of people is by telling myself I will be responsible for taking my body along but spirit will have to do the rest. My guides have never failed me.

I looked down on the sea of faces in the hall that night, and thought it would be my first and last appearance. There were several of us doing readings from flowers handed in by people in the crowd. When it was my turn to do the clairvoyance demonstration, I was shaking so badly I had to hold onto the rostrum.

I remember looking at Mum's face and then at Bob's as I took the first flower. The next thing I remember is that there were no flowers left in the box. Suddenly the whole roomful of people converged on me with congratulations, and a bombardment of questions and requests for more information on their readings. The session had lasted for two and a half hours; it was two more hours before I was able to leave.

When we got home, I was drained of energy and yet I couldn't sleep. It is a wonderful feeling to be able to help people with the gifts given me, and I felt God wanted me to do this work. So many people were excited because they had seen my guide's face superimposed on my own. Some had received survival evidence from loved ones, and others had been given messages that helped solve their particular problems.

I continued to give public demonstrations, and I still do. These days, they are often in clubs, where people can sit and feel at ease with their friends. The entry fee is low, so anybody who feels the need or the interest can afford to come.

My friend, the radio broadcaster Suzy Yates, comperes these demonstrations. She begins by asking people (before I come on stage) to write down requests in one of two categories: either for information about their own future; or for survival evidence from a loved one who has passed on. The pieces of paper are put into two different barrels, depending on the nature of the request. Five flowers are also distributed at random.

Suzy then introduces me, and I give a short talk about why I do these shows. I explain that I am an educator, and that I will use any available means to educate people about psychic ability: how it can be used to pass on advice, gentle (or not-so-gentle) reprimands, and any other messages that those in spirit wish to give to their loved ones here on earth.

Survival evidence proves to the people who receive it, and others who witness this, that there is no death. It takes away the fear, and brings great comfort to those who have lost loved ones, or who are facing the prospect of imminent death themselves.

Messages about the future often help people to understand their own intuitive knowledge, which they may have been resisting. The wisdom and advice passed on by those in spirit who love us can help people change their lives in positive and wonderful ways.

As the shows proceed, I take pieces of paper from each barrel and give readings. When people in the audience recognise their loved ones from the messages, they put their hands up so that I can go and talk to them in more depth, and pass on other messages.

From the five flowers that have been handed out, I do flower readings, mainly to honour the memory of the pioneers of spiritualism.

Here are just a couple of examples of readings done at club shows in Australia.

An older lady wrote that she wanted to know if her father was still alive. She had been told by two other clairvoyants that he was. She also wrote that her father had gone to war more than forty years earlier. As I read her note from the barrel, I felt sad at what I saw. Her father had, in fact, died very early on in the war. I described to her how he had been killed. I then went on to give her the proof she needed: a description of a tall, thin, moustached, fine-looking young man in a grey uniform with long black boots and a black hat. The woman was shocked but convinced, as this was exactly how her father had looked in his European army uniform the day he left for the war. I was able to tell her that proof of his death would arrive soon. Some months later, she wrote to let me know that she had received in the mail official documentation confirming his death, in the manner I had described.

At another club demonstration, a very young woman handed me the flower she had been holding, and asked what direction she should take in her life. I could see immediately that for the past two years she had been mixing with a group of people who were a very negative influence on her, and who had been making her life (and that of her mother) miserable. I told her this, and she admitted to being very scared. I was also able to tell her that she had a resilient nature, and that she should break all ties with those 'friends' who were closest to her, because they were in fact taking advantage of her generosity. I advised her to forget the wrongs of the past two years, make new friends, and move on in her life in a positive direction. The mother was visibly relieved – and so was the young woman. She had received the confirmation she needed to turn her life around.

Another area of my work over the years has been rescue work – clearing houses or buildings of spirits who are 'stuck' in the lower astral. When people feel they are being 'haunted', it is often because a spirit, unable to move on, is making its presence known in a range of ways that can't be explained in rational terms. Naturally, most people find this disconcerting, and even frightening.

Working out what is going on, and helping the troubled spirit to move on, can be very hard work and can take several visits. For a long time, I did this kind of clearing work, usually with a friend, and didn't charge. As the years went by, however, I gathered a group of people, trained them, gave the name 'rescue work' to this phenomenon (it is now the accepted term) and kept taped records of every case we handled.

When I first started, a friend and I would go into the affected house or business premises and I would go into trance. Then the spirit entity causing trouble for the occupants would use my body to communicate with my friend. She would question the person to find out why he or she was earthbound and would talk and pray, immersing the entity in white light. In most cases it worked, but it is by no means a straightforward procedure.

Certainly there are earthbound spirits, but as we dealt with this area in depth, we became aware of another problem. Quite a few people have over-active imaginations and attribute something as normal as fluttering curtains to a spirit haunting them. Others have psychological difficulties and want to believe they are possessed, while still others just want attention or publicity.

So we learnt through our experiences. It didn't take too long for me to cultivate and enlist another member into our group of people who could give professional help: a psychiatrist, who is a wonderful person, always ready and able to help those I can persuade to see her.

Here is one example of fairly recent rescue work where there definitely was an earthbound spirit.

Not long after I began working in radio, I was at the offices of a major Sydney station to prepare for a forthcoming show. One by one, people began approaching me with stories of strange happenings in the building. The lights on an entire floor would flash on and off – and yet no fault was found in the wiring, and no one was flicking the switches. Heavy fire doors would bang in stairwells, and yet no one had been in the stairwell at the time. Not surprisingly, many of the staff were feeling scared and very concerned.

As I began to investigate what might be going on, a young man in the production department confided that a close friend of his had recently committed suicide. The young man felt guilty because he believed he should have been able to help his friend. It turned out that the friend was indeed trying to contact the young man, not to chide him, but to reassure him that he had been in no way responsible, and to say how sorry he was for the grief he had caused by his suicide.

As I spoke to this troubled spirit, I was able to reassure him that I would pass on his message, and persuade him that it was time for him to move on. I talked gently with him for some time, until he was able to see the brilliant white light, and decided to move towards it. Needless to say, there were no more strange happenings in the building after that.

෴

For a number of years now, I have had radio shows in Australia and the USA, where my main work is to give survival evidence. People call the station and the operator puts them through to us in the studio.

When a caller makes contact with a loved one, it can be a highly emotional program. Tears of joy, frustration and anguish flow. But because we have a listening audience, the program must keep going. The broadcaster's expertise keeps the program from floundering at times when words fail; it's not always easy to keep one's composure. It can be overwhelming for everyone when you are continually hearing the proof given that people do survive that transition called death.

How do I make contact with the spirit world in these situations? From the time I leave home to drive to the radio station, which in Sydney takes about twenty minutes, I am aware of spirit people gathering around me. I always drive because it keeps my conscious mind occupied. (If I were a passenger, I would be relaxed and in a receptive state of mind. This would allow spirit voices to bombard me with images and impressions that can present problems when I need to focus during my radio broadcast.) When I start driving, I use a process that I call a trigger. I recite or sing in my mind a particular song to block out as much interference as possible to my subconscious mind. It is not unlike a post-hypnotic suggestion. And I always try to drive over the same route.

During the program I rely on a process of letting spirit personalities access and impress my subconscious, so I need to be as clear and calm as possible. We have so many people phoning in, and I am usually on air for just under two hours, so we are limited in the number of calls we can accept. When I arrive at the radio station, I use a process to tune the broadcaster to the spirit world. This helps them to be more open to the messages coming through from the spirit communicators.

And there are always so many spirit people waiting in the studio when I arrive, it is like a football stadium. Once a caller is on air, the announcer asks two questions: 'How long ago did the person die?' and, 'What is your relationship to that person?' Because the program is happening as the audience is listening, I need the time those questions give me to assimilate what I am receiving from the spirit world. The vibration of the caller's voice also enables me to get a clearer, quicker communication. There is no process of 'calling up the dead'. The spirit people are already waiting excitedly to get a message through to those they care about.

I had been doing radio work in Australia for some time when I was asked to do survival evidence for the Danny Bonaduce Radio Program in Chicago, USA. The amazing advances of modern technology make it possible for me to sit in my home in Australia and talk via the telephone to people in America, where the push of a button on their radios brings my voice into the homes, cars and workplaces of millions of people.

The following are examples from one of my radio shows in Australia.

Rick rang our program wanting a message from his grandmother. The first thing she said was, 'Tell him I'm with his mother. She was there to meet me when I entered the spirit world.'

Rick was ecstatic. 'I prayed they would be together,' he replied. She continued giving her grandson undeniable proof that she was happy in her new world. Laughing, she said, 'Tell him my hair is still red.' 'That would be right,' replied Rick, explaining that his grandmother was eighty-four years old when she died and it had been a longstanding joke between them that regardless of how she felt, every month she would go to the hairdresser and have her hair coloured red. He was the one who used to drive her to the hairdresser's in the later years and he had always said to her, 'I'm never going to have a grey-haired grandmother.' She had always replied, 'I just hope they have hairdressers in the next world.'

Another caller, Alan, wanted a message from his father, who had died three months earlier. 'He's in an army uniform and there are two men, also in army uniforms, standing beside him. The names John, James and Bill are being given to me,' I said. Alan replied, 'John is Dad's name, James is his brother and Bill was a friend he grew up with, who died in the Second World War. Dad loved his brother James and often told me how much he missed them both.' I told Alan that I saw John holding his hand out to show me a medal. It was bronze in colour, with a ribbon attached to it. Alan replied that he couldn't make any sense out of that: 'Dad never talked about his army days; all I know was that he was a prisoner of war. Whenever I questioned him about those days he always said, "I want to forget".' John (Alan's father) then produced a packet of tobacco with the name 'Capstan' written on the cover, and started rolling a cigarette. As I was relaying this to Alan, he started laughing and said, 'Oh, yes! Dad always insisted on rolling his own cigarettes, and Capstan is the brand he used.' John continued to give messages to his son that he could understand. As we concluded, we both agreed that it was strange for a man who had never wanted to be reminded of his army days to present himself in uniform holding a medal that he didn't own when he was alive.

This is an extract from a letter I later received from Alan: 'Imagine my surprise when I received a letter informing me that my father was to be decorated at a ceremony to take place at Government House. How proud I felt standing there as they handed me his medal. I knew that he, James and Bill were standing beside me. Everything fell into place about the uniform and medal when I received that letter. The medal is sitting beside his picture on my mantelpiece.'

⌘

Aside from the public demonstrations and radio work, I continue to give private readings and to teach others how to use their psychic abilities. In an environment of confidentiality and with enough time, readings can be deeper and give more intimate details of the relationship an entity had with family and friends when they were alive. With public demonstrations, especially radio broadcasts, the messages must be quick and to the point; lack of time often does not permit deeper, more spiritual insights to be given.

Whatever the context, however, listening to people giving messages from the spirit world has something of value for everyone. It does not have to be someone you know for you to benefit. The messages can be either heart-breaking, extremely sad, uplifting or very funny. I have received many letters of thanks from the listening audience after doing public demonstrations and radio work. Many people don't need to call the radio station when I'm demonstrating my abilities. It's enough for them to hear the caller receive the proof that their loved one has survived death.

In my private practice, the reading is recorded on audio tape for the client. When the tape is played for the client's family members and friends, it is common for me to receive a letter or thank-you note saying that they, too, were uplifted and can now proceed more happily with their lives.

In the following chapters, I have explained some of the insights and teachings I have gained over the years through these various aspects of my work, and through my communication with the spirit world.

Remember – what I can do, you can do. I hope that as you read on, questions will be answered, and understandings will be clarified.

PART 2

$\mathcal{I}$NSIGHTS

5

*O*UR JOURNEY
BACK TO EARTH

WHETHER OR NOT WE REALISE IT, life is an ongoing cycle of birth and death. It is a wonderful journey, designed to help each and every soul learn and grow in love and light. The soul is the indestructible part of us that continues on from life to life and death to death. It's the part of us that has memory of everything from our first life to where we are now. It supersedes time, space and intellectual knowledge. Instead, it holds true knowledge, knowledge we have acquired throughout many lives, as well as the knowledge we've acquired between lives when we're in the spirit dimensions.

The ultimate goal is to be in contact with our soul and its vast store of knowledge. This is part of the journey through lifetimes.

So, how do we move from life to life? Certainly the spirit world is our home and between lives on earth, we return home. Before our birth, before conception even, we are shown the basic structure for our lives. We are given choices as to the broad circumstances of our lives, such as our parents, our sex and our race. We then agree to the basic events that will shape our learning on earth for our life to come.

Once we're back on earth, the choices as to what we do with these circumstances are ours to decide. Some of us choose to move on from the circumstances of our early lives, while others prefer to remain with these conditions. Either way there is always free will. The opportunities or limitations that follow result from the choices we make.

Each of us comes with a mission to fulfil, with a definite and unique purpose. In some lives we achieve very little or nothing. In other lives we make great headway. No matter how hard the going gets, there are always opportunities for us, however faint they might appear. There are always guides to help us, when we're ready, on our way.

Once we've agreed to the basic circumstances of our lives, conception can take place. Choosing to incarnate is like lining up for the helter skelter, and once on the slide we can't get off. The course of events is now set in motion. We've been conceived and are on our journey back to earth. It's only then we start to remember the limitations and difficulties of human life.

The journey through conception and birth is the reverse to that of death. It is a soul's journey from the world of spirit back to the earth plane. From the magical moment of conception and during the months of pregnancy, the spirit is attached to the mother and moves backwards and forwards from the heavier vibrations of earth to its spirit home. This movement to and fro is necessary to allow the soul to adapt to the far denser energies of our earth environment.

While only an embryo, the soul starts to gather information about its new home and begins a process of assimilation. It becomes aware of the wider conditions on earth at the time – wars, interactions between nations, the spiritual mood of the times and so on. It experiences its mother's feelings and emotions.

At this time the embryo's aura is blending with the auras of its parents. Through the auras of its parents, the soul is aware of its wider surroundings and of the energy of the people its parents associate with. It knows about conversations between friends and relatives of the parents, even though they aren't close by. All this is part of the soul's assimilation process into the earth plane. The information gathered is then stored away in the child's subconscious for later reference.

From conception to birth, as the soul goes through this process of conditioning and making the transition from spirit to earth, it moves backwards and forwards between the two planes with ease. It's like having our mind in two places at one time. We're aware of both spirit and earth places, but can only concentrate on one at a time. We have a sense of the growth of our baby body and of our parents' world and, through this, an objective awareness begins to develop.

When it comes time for birth to begin, it happens in a split second. In that instant, the split consciousness between the earth and spirit planes disappears, and the baby is now totally contained within its earth body. It feels a great excitement at the thought of finally being born. The baby realises the need to leave its mother and struggle out into the light. It puts all its energy into getting down the dark birth channel – and this journey can be painful. What greets the baby when it is finally born is the incredible light and the noise. Its first experience of the physical world is discomfort and hunger but, as always, it's also an adventure for the soul.

Few parents understand the assimilation process their baby is experiencing, but life becomes much easier once they do. Basically, it takes five years from the time of birth for the spiritual and psychic forces of a child's nature to balance with the physical, emotional and mental aspects of their personalities. When this balance is achieved, children have clear access to the higher self, although their experiences in the earth plane inhibit their ability to maintain this clear access. As we grow older, many of us lose our awareness of the connection altogether.

The soul's process of assimilation from the world of spirit into this world is an extremely delicate one. And so it's essential that children be allowed to go through this process at their own pace. A child is pure; pure spirit has to learn to adapt to the limitations and the heavier vibrations of the earth plane. This can be particularly hard for the children whose memory of spirit is very strong and who feel the earth plane alien to them.

Parents can do a great deal to cherish children in this regard. They need to know that all children are psychic. It's the influence of the adults and environment they grow up in that dictates how long a child's spiritual eyes remain open. I can't stress how important it is for us to allow children to be their normal selves and to accept their own private worlds without question or ridicule. If the adult world that surrounds the child is dominated by material needs, then the child will grow up with no time for spiritual truths. And, if everything that the parents can't understand or see gets classed as childish imagination or fantasy, the child will conform to this view and bury their natural psychic tendencies.

A young child's subconscious mind is so open and pliable, their level of receptivity can be amazing. Often they see auras around people and pets. And where they don't see auras, they do all feel and sense energy. Because of this incredible ability to absorb what is around them, it is important to monitor what happens to our children, and to provide them with a positive environment free from violence and aggression.

Children are relatively new to the energies and attitudes of this world. Their psychic faculties are wide open and their subconscious mind is in an acutely receptive state, uncluttered by fears and prejudices. Because of this openness it's easy for the child's spiritual eyes to accept the happenings and events of the spiritual dimensions that are taking place on earth.

Concepts of earthly time, for example, have not yet impregnated the child's memory, and so earthly limitations have not taken root. The story of the imaginary playmate or of a deceased relative being seen is common and the child accepts these happenings without question and believes this to be normal, until told otherwise.

Normally, when children are looking at a tray full of caterpillars, they're likely to think that one day these furry caterpillars will be beautiful butterflies. However, if on a movie or on television they've seen the caterpillars turn into menacing, ugly monsters, caterpillars are no longer viewed as a beautiful part of nature, but as horrible creatures to be feared. Their imaginations override the spiritual message of transformation with something scary.

Such injections of horror and violence warp their life view early on and rob them of the knowledge of the light they have brought from their spirit home. We must do everything we can to work on the positive, to show them that the world is a safe place. Once fear takes root, it narrows our wider spiritual experiences as adults as well.

Often I see this when people come to me for readings. They come to me saying they desperately want to see a loved one. Although I can't say anything, I know, in fact, that they're afraid to see. Even some of my students, well along the path of development, have the same problem. They have worked hard and yet their clairvoyant faculties are not developing. Again, this is because they are afraid to see. They are unable to progress until we go back to that incident in childhood where the fear began.

Children are immensely receptive to their environment. This receptivity can often explain their unexpected response to a family member or friend. Take Aunt Cathy, for example, who visits her sister's home every Tuesday night and stays for supper. Much to everyone's embarrassment, her niece doesn't want to kiss her aunt. She doesn't want to be held by her or to be anywhere near this adult. The child cannot explain that when her aunt comes into the house, the energy she brings with her is one of hate, anger, fear, death, sickness and suffering.

When asked by her parents to respond to this loving relative, the child's only defence is to give some of the anger and confusion back. She might say she doesn't like her aunt and doesn't want to kiss her. She might run into another room or disrupt the visit in any way she can, because she is afraid something terrible is going to happen. Either way, the whole experience ends up being unsatisfactory for everyone, and the evening probably ends with the child being told she's a naughty girl and getting sent to bed.

The funny thing is that Aunt Cathy also visits her sister once a month on a Sunday. During these visits, the child will kiss her aunt and even sometimes make a fuss of her. The confused family members put this inconsistent behaviour down to the child's moods, because no one has ever linked the relevant facts. The reality is that from Monday to Friday, Cathy works in the emergency room at the local hospital. She comes straight from work on Tuesdays to have dinner at her niece's home. She is a compassionate person, it transpires, with a particularly sensitive nature. She often feels the pain of the patients she cares for. Her job is not just a job, it's a calling; so it's normal for her to be preoccupied when she leaves work with all the things that happened in her day. Pain and suffering are a normal part of that work, but Cathy has no idea that her energy field, her aura, has absorbed all those negative conditions.

The child cannot reason these feelings out any more than the adults can, nor is she able to disassociate from the unpleasant emotions she feels. She thinks all those negative energies are being sent from her aunt to her. Sundays simply don't have the same emotions and negativity because Aunt Cathy isn't coming from work when she visits, and so everyone's happy. If only we understood this wider perspective, how much easier it would be for everyone.

The interesting thing is that if children are allowed to progress normally without negative bombardment from television or aggressive behaviour from adults, they usually won't be afraid of the dark. That's because they are in a safe and nurturing environment.

Sometimes, though, a child may have nightmares and it is difficult for a parent to ascertain where the problem lies. What I have come to learn about nightmares is that we should never force children to sleep in a dark room if they're having problems. This only reinforces their fear, and their imagination takes over, making things worse.

As a parent, it is hard to know when the nightmare is a product of the child's own fear and when it is from the spirit world. Your children might well be having nightmares because they are seeing people in spirit and are frightened of them in the same way they might be afraid of meeting any other stranger. Introduce them to this person in spirit and explain that the person loves them; this allows them to make a conscious connection with that person. They are then able to go into sleep feeling protected and safe.

If a child is particularly prone to nightmares, the parent can help a great deal by lightening the atmosphere before bedtime. Allow the little one to watch or listen to an uplifting story; that way, you'll lighten the surrounding energy. If, having done all that, the child is still having nightmares, find out what the nightmares are about. It's important to allow the child to go into detail, because it's only through this detail that the answers will tend to emerge. As you're listening, ascertain how much of what is taking place during the child's day is contributing to the uneasy dreams. You might find it was a video or something disturbing on the news, or even a snippet overheard from an adult conversation. Acknowledge the child's fears and concerns, and provide lots of love and comfort. Leave a night light or small candle burning in the room until they are asleep.

In other cases, where a child is highly strung and has become disturbed by outside influences, fear may take root in the subconscious, causing an imbalance. The subconscious mind becomes so stimulated that the child becomes hyperactive and unable to play happily alone. Such children don't want to let the adult they feel safe with out of sight. They're afraid to sleep, so they fight it. A pattern emerges. No amount of disciplinary action is getting the required response, and the despairing parents start to think they are living in a different world to that of their child.

On the other hand, it's common for sensitive children to go into themselves, to become quiet and distant, to lack concentration and lose interest in things taking place around them. When questioned about their behaviour, these children will tend to reply that they're bored, because they cannot put into words the fact that they're preoccupied with the voices they hear, with the constant pictures running through their minds, with the colours and feelings that are so confusing to them because their outer world is so at odds with their inner experiences. The parents are totally unaware that this conflict is sapping the child's mental energy. In trying to interpret their own reality, the children describe this process as daydreaming or as being bored.

It's not only parents without spiritual or psychic understanding who fail to give their children the respect they deserve. I've met a number of new age mothers who want their children to be especially psychic and they try their very best to influence and hasten their children's development. Either way, the child feels pressured and confused.

When children develop normally, through everyday experiences of their own, they learn to assimilate their psychic experiences with situations in their everyday lives. This process of association of psychic impressions and energies as interpreted by the child is not always correct. This process continues to a greater or lesser extent throughout life. Parents cannot order this assimilation for their children, but they can help enormously by the environment they create for their little ones.

So, we simply need to treat our children with love, gentleness and respect, for the path they've chosen for themselves in this life is a unique one. We should not interfere with this path but rather encourage them to explore all those things, that spiritual knowledge, bedded deep inside of them.

It is helpful if parents understand that the child has help from the world of spirit. The child might, for example, be aware of a little spirit friend like my Mary, who will manifest as a playmate, who will appear as substantial as the rest of us and who will teach the child in their early years. The child might have an animal spirit who is a constant companion. How many times have you heard friends talk about a child's 'imaginary' pets?

All this can be a bit disconcerting for a parent, but it needn't be. There's no need to intrude into this relationship. Simply treat it with respect and provide a nurturing environment for it to take its own course. Allowing your children the space to play alone with their thoughts, to be alone with nature in their own backyard is ideal. Providing this sort of environment is essential if children are to achieve a good balance between their spiritual nature and that part of their nature that connects them to the earth dimension.

Childhood can still be a truly magical experience and this is due in part to the fact that much is available to children because of their purity. Jesus's saying that we have to become as a child to enter the Kingdom of Heaven has a greater depth than perhaps we'd realised.

∽

As I have said, it is very important to protect our children from violent and negative experiences for as long as possible. Our world at present has many areas of darkness and negativity, which can be very frightening. I see among our young people so much reluctance to incarnate. This happens to a whole range of souls and has nothing to do with being suicidal. Rather, it's as if part of them isn't quite all here. These are the reluctant souls. Instead of walking and talking quickly to get out of the baby stage, they'll stay as long as they can. They haven't accepted the responsibility of being back, and so are ill at ease about returning to earth.

As children, these souls are either rebellious or highly dependent. Still, because their subconscious is very receptive, they need to be treated with care. The over-stimulation of these sorts of children will only make them worse. The imbalance between the spiritual and the physical frequently causes a biochemical imbalance in the body that can manifest as severe allergies – just another way of rebelling about being here. In such cases, good diets and nurturing surroundings are essential to bring these children into balance.

There's a simple explanation for this. No matter the type of individual, we all become bored with doing the same thing and being in the same environment, even in the spirit world. And when we are between lives in spirit, sooner or later the desire surfaces to explore some more. This desire brings about the circumstances that end with incarnation into another life.

We become very excited at the prospect of a new adventure back on earth, having, of course, forgotten about the realities of life on this plane as compared to our existence in the spirit world. And, as time has little meaning in the spirit world, the prospect of seventy or eighty years back on earth doesn't seem too hard a task at all. As far as we're concerned, it'll pass in the blink of an eye.

Reality hits us, however, from the moment of our conception. From that instant, we are attached through our mother's energy field to this earth dimension with its whirlwind thoughts and events, its turmoil and its heavier energy which we absorb, reminding us once more of other times we were incarnate.

Some souls then want to change their mind, but can't. The course of events is now set in motion. They've been conceived and are on their journey back to earth. For a lot of people, this whole process is a terrifying experience. They want to abort before they're even born. These souls come into the world with noticeable attitudes and patterns; for example, they sleep longer hours, they tend to be the dreamers and the sleepwalkers. Often they are unsettled, highly sensitive babies who can't adjust to eating and sleeping. They need a lot of patience and understanding and demand a lot from their parents.

If this baby grows into a child who still has sleep problems, it is a good idea to check whether they have a medical problem preventing good sleep. We certainly can't attribute everything to the spirit world. That done, if the child has been close to a relative who is deceased, place a photo of that relative by their bed. Say that this loved one is now the child's guardian angel and will protect the child from anything scary. If they haven't known anyone deceased, introduce them to the photo of a deceased loved one and do the same thing. You might wonder how all this works. Each one of us has loved ones in spirit and, because your child is part of you, they love your child as an extension of you. They are only too happy to watch over your beloved little one during sleep.

It is also important to remember that a child is just as receptive to negative vibrations and information as they are to positive ones. How positive or negative aspects will be expressed in the sleep state depends on personality and environment.

These early years are so very precious. From five onwards, children are busy learning about this world, assimilating their environment and absorbing the lessons taught by parents and school. To share the magical world of early childhood is a great gift for all involved. We don't have to have all the answers and, in fact, there is a great deal to learn from our little ones, if only we had the time to listen. In cases where the spirituality and psychic tendencies of the child have been nurtured, achieving a balance in their physical and emotional natures, you can witness some outstanding examples of the continuity of the soul.

Often children will talk about previous lives they have lived with people they have known from those lives and who are now a part of their new existence. There are numerous documented cases of children giving details of the countries, cities and towns in which they've lived; the names of former relatives; descriptions of their previous homes, and much more. Again and again we get this information, which can be authenticated and which proves without doubt that they lived before.

When I was a child it was often the adults in my life who would trigger my psychic nature. I was lucky, because then they would follow through from what I said. As they asked questions, more information would come through for me.

I well remember an incident when my little sister was three years old. Mum was driving along a country road and we were chatting away; my sister was sitting in the back of the car. At one point we saw a notice on the side of the road advertising mushrooms for sale. 'Oh, mushrooms, fifty-nine cents a pound,' my little sister said – although, of course, at three she was too young to be able to read.

We were amazed. But at that moment, there was no separation between my tiny sister's spiritual self and the child on the earth plane. While the child might still be small and unable to read, write, or articulate, their spirit is wise, ancient and all-knowing. In situations like this, take the opportunity to let the child talk. This enables them to access that wiser part of themselves.

Another example of the remarkable aspects of childhood is children's ability to heal themselves, especially of the cuts, bruises and burns that are commonly associated with growing up. When we're in the spirit world, we're taught about energies and how to work with them for many purposes, including healing. And so, until life is complicated for us back on the earth plane, we can in fact access this spiritual awareness. It is second nature to us.

Only when people tell children these things can't be done does it become impossible, because doubt and fear creep in. Instinctively, the child knows it can heal itself. Adult fears are what impede this natural instinct. Panic about how bad a cut might be or how easily a child might have been permanently damaged doesn't help. When we do this, we transmit the pain, anxiety and panic to the child, who then comes to associate pain and injury with fear.

As parents, we need to cherish the purity and spiritual aware-ness of childhood. Allow children to grow in a positive and loving environment, so that they can follow the path they have chosen for this lifetime.

6

THE ADVENTURE OF LIFE

TIME PASSES, WE GROW UP and our view of life alters. Too often we lose the magic and freshness of childhood. Some days we can feel very jaded with life, but really we are so lucky. Often we complain that we've never won anything. When we're in this frame of mind, we're off course. The very fact that we're here on earth proves we're winners. Whether we realise it or not, we've won the trip of a lifetime, the chance to come back to earth to learn and to grow. I can't tell you how many souls there are who are waiting for their opportunity to get back here and have another shot at earthly existence.

But we're not sent here and then left completely to our own devices, not unless we want to be. There is always assistance for us, when we ask for it with a sincere heart. We have our guides.

People are often curious about guides, asking what they are like. How does this relationship come about? Well, again, it's all down to our free will. Before any soul incarnates it makes an agreement with a guide or guides to help each other during the incarnating soul's next lifetime.

Just as we all have friends, everyone has a guide in the spirit world. Our guides are there to help and guide us. If we go into an area of service for others, for example, we add to our team of guides, because we need to call on more help to enable us to do our work well. If we specialise in an area, guides come our way with the specialist knowledge we're needing at that time. Some of us have been guides to other people between incarnations.

How do we know when guides are around? Well, everyone has a unique energy field (aura) around them, whether they are living or dead. Through our aura, we recognise that our guides are around. We will feel this as an unusual sensation in our body. It might be a shiver or shudder, for example, that alerts us to their presence. And then, because their presence is so familiar to us, we don't need to ask who it is. The communication with our guides is much quicker and more precise than when we rely on our psychic senses or intuition.

What's happening when our guide draws close is a touching or blending of auras. With a guide around, we know we're never alone, even for a moment, although we are frequently left alone with our own thinking process so that we can make our own decisions. Our guides are there to point us in the right direction on our search through life.

What is the process like? It's like holding the hand of a child who is learning to walk. Once the child has learned to walk, we step back and allow them to walk on their own. Our guides don't necessarily stop us falling on every occasion, but they are always there to pick us up.

Similarly, when we are in a situation that makes us feel uncertain, if we allow them, our guides can shepherd us through. They come to us as that still small voice which, sadly, we often disregard, preferring to be dictated to by our logic.

When I was a child, my spirit guide Mary came to me in the form of a child, so I could relate to her. When I was older and developing my skills as a medium, Mary came to me as an older medium. She did this to give me the confidence that comes with having an older person around as a teacher. Mary still comes to me as an older woman and still often dresses in different outfits.

These days Mary mainly acts as a guiding influence when I'm conducting services. She is very useful because in her former life she was a Scottish spiritualist medium. Throughout the years she has been spotted by many who are developing their psychic powers, as well as by other mediums, who ask me about the bonneted round-faced, blue-eyed lady wearing gloves and carrying a handbag.

Mary has a strong accent and a type of humour very different from mine. When I'm getting a message with her help, the language I use is hers. Mary certainly has a no-nonsense way of telling things. She manifests so strongly that when I'm working, not infrequently those around me no longer see me – they only see Mary.

Another dear guide is Chang Tao, a former Chinese mandarin, who has been with me from the moment I took my first breath in this life and who will remain at my side until I breathe my last. All the other guides who help me in my work do so through his instruction. Chang Tao and I have lived lives together for centuries. He has an incredible sense of humour and when he uses me in trance, his way of talking is very clipped and distinctive.

He is a very loving spirit. However, there are times when we do not see eye to eye. As in any other relationship, there are times when he tells me things I don't want to hear, and other times when his silence prevails, although I feel he should be talking to me. I've never discussed our disagreements with anyone and yet, over the years, I've had calls from other mediums with a message for me from Chang. Initially, they thought it was because I was too busy for Chang to get through at the time; now they know it's likely we've had a disagreement.

Chang is at all times a teaching guide. Over the years I have taught many who have themselves become teachers and have gone on to teach others. There are occasions when Chang has helped my students with something they needed to learn. I'm the only medium he channels through, however.

Like all guides, Chang has to lower his vibration to be able to work within the earth plane; and for him it's an uncomfortable process. However, it is a two-way process. We learn from our guides and they learn by being a close part of our earth experience. Their learning comes through observing us as we

live our lives. As each personality is unique, so are the opportunities to learn. We may, for example, choose to swim the river;
had it been left up to our guide, he or she might have preferred
to walk around the river. By understanding the reasoning power
we've used, they benefit from this experience.

When I first became aware that I could ask my guides for help
and information, I got a few surprises. Many of my questions
would be answered in parables. I hated this process and still do.
It is mostly visual, but it can sometimes be verbal. When I asked
questions about my own future or the outcome of a particular
situation, I would be given or shown different scenarios, depending on which path I chose to follow. I was never given the
answer, and was always told that I had to think for myself. And,
I was reminded, if I didn't make my own decisions, I was not
progressing, because I wasn't using my own free will.

Ultimately, the whole purpose of these experiences, some
easier than others, is to help us become completely one with our
higher spiritual nature. This means we get to the stage where
we don't have to ask questions all the time because we have a
deep sense of knowing.

This doesn't mean to say we know the outcome of a good
deal of what we do. But whatever direction we take, whatever
choice we make, no matter how adverse a situation it might
seem, still we know deep inside ourselves we are on the right
track. Things can appear to be very bad but we know in ourselves that this terrible time will pass, and that we can only grow
from this difficult experience. We come to understand that there
are no absolute certainties in this life and that we need to have
courage to learn from our life situations.

If the decisions were made for us throughout life, we'd never
reach this point of inner understanding. Each lesson is about
having the courage to step forward, even though we don't quite
know where it is we're being taken. Fear, on the other hand, is
the basis of so many wrong decisions we make in life.

I remember at one stage, for example, I just couldn't come
to terms with the story of Sodom and Gomorrah. How, I won-
dered, could a loving God destroy His people? I was shown the

situation over a number of weeks and each time I revisited Sodom and Gomorrah, I would see the situation from multiple perspectives. The resulting destruction of these cities, I learned, was due to the abuse of knowledge.

So we can take comfort in knowing that our loving and compassionate guides are always with us. When we learn to tune in to our higher spiritual self, and have the courage to use our free will wisely, our life, and the lives of those around us, is rich and rewarding.

So, we have guides from spirit and we also have plenty of daily help in this world, even if it's just the kind word or the warm smile on the day we're feeling down. Or it might be a book we buy or a helpful article we come across in a paper or magazine. All these things are gifts to help lighten the load, when things are feeling a bit tough. Too often we don't realise just what help we're being given.

Even in the beautiful world of Nature that surrounds and uplifts us, we have beings whose job it is to care for the natural kingdom, which in turn can heal us and give us peace in times of strife. These helpers are the fairy folk.

෴

This brings us to the question of the fairy kingdom. In recent times there's been a resurgence of interest in fairies. Fairies, or nature spirits, are as old as time itself. If we were able to talk to family members a few generations back many of us, regardless of race, would be amazed at the personal stories they can recount. My own Irish roots are steeped in a deep love and respect for the fairy kingdom, and even today the Irish have a rich treasure trove of such stories to draw upon.

Whenever anyone talks about a fairy, they are immediately uplifted, because there is a definite positive healing energy that comes with this thought. Children see fairies more because they have no reason to disbelieve what they see. The fairies have a very pure, light energy and, since children are also very pure, they are far more able to access that dimension. It's important we don't cut them off from this reality.

I'm often asked what the fairies are like. Different fairies have different jobs to do. Like the rest of creation, each is unique. They have differing personalities just as we humans have and, like the human race, fairies come in different shapes and sizes and genders. By their very nature fairies are like butterflies, flitting from flower to flower.

Fairies are the caretakers of our natural world. Their main task is to enhance the vibrations of each flower, plant and tree; in so doing, they also enhance the natural colours of the plant kingdom. We in turn benefit from this work.

Take, for example, the colour green, which is a natural healing vibration that we all need, mostly for our emotional nature. When we expose ourselves to the green of nature in trees, we are receiving not only oxygen for our bodies but also oxygen for our souls. The healing greens open us up spiritually as well as physically and help us breathe. Just as the gardener tends the garden so that it is beautiful for the eye to see, the nature spirits are the unseen workers who balance the energies of nature.

When we tamper with nature, by creating pollution, for example, there is nothing these nature spirits can do except to impress on those of us who are likely to be receptive the importance of the environment.

Because of their light energy, fairies are unable to tolerate the heavy vibrations of our cities and will enter them only for a specific task. Whether a person is developing their psychic awareness or not, they still might catch a glimpse of fairy folk as a flicker or pinprick of light that has no apparent source. Theirs is not a light of this dimension. When we do see the fairy 'lights', we are glimpsing their life force, which illuminates this world, lighting up the dark corners. Part of the task of fairy folk is to awaken the consciousness of humankind and of all the creatures great and small that inhabit the planet.

We are in need of this consciousness more than ever before. Before the advent of radio we were not so assaulted by the more oppressive vibrations of contemporary life. Previously, we made our own music, we talked together, but we also had a great deal of time for silence, to be alone with ourselves and our own thoughts. Our new generations have almost no silence. They are receiving constant bombardment with savage and fearful messages.

Years ago, as they walked the tightrope of adolescence, teenagers could draw strength from the old stories they had been told, stories of faith and hope and magic. And so, as they grew up, they were able to retain an expectation that no matter how difficult life might be at times, magic might still happen. Now, children and adolescents are assaulted by a weight of information, a barrage of negative music and a popular culture that offers so little that is hopeful. This is something we as adults and parents must be aware of.

So, how does the timeless wisdom projected from the fairy realms touch our lives? We receive it visually. For example, pictures are projected throughout the universe of a planet without trees. This picture is picked up by everyone's subconscious mind. However, it is only children and sensitive adults who will consciously understand the message and the warning: our trees are being logged; we might end up with a planet without trees.

Steven Spielberg's *Close Encounters of the Third Kind* is an excellent example of what I mean. We see people going about their everyday lives, then home in on a man in his pick-up truck. All the electrics in the truck start to play up. Then, as the man looks up, he sees a flying saucer and follows it to a hill where hundreds of people are gathering to watch the flying saucers. Here his subconscious mind is impressed with information as to where a future meeting will take place.

This man becomes obsessive about trying to recreate what he saw, first with a drawing, then as a sculpture. He can't work because he is obsessed with his project and even tries to create a replica of the mountain in dirt in his lounge room.

Many people, we discover, are going through the same process. Some recognised the mountain almost at once, so there's no problem for them. Then the hero gets a clue during a TV interview. He spots the mountain and takes off, not knowing exactly why he has to be there. All those who follow their impulse and make it to the mountain, having been drawn there from all over the country, experience a wonderful exchange between life forms. The experience changes forever their view of the world and of how they are to live in it.

The fairy kingdom (the nature spirits) implant messages to help the natural world. Many people, sadly, discount the messages that come to them as thoughts or impressions. Others act on what they are given and fight to save the whales and the rainforests.

Now, not all of us are going to feel so 'in tune' with our guides or whatever. Often when we need guidance most, we feel most confused. We want to have answers to the questions in our lives that are plaguing us. Too often we want *easy* answers. We just want life to get better, without really understanding that there are lessons we need to learn from the situation in which we find ourselves.

We might have been taken advantage of at work and are feeling so stressed we no longer know what to do. We blame everything on our boss and pray that he or she will leave. The lesson for us in this situation, however, might be learning to say no or learning our own worth. Whether the boss comes or goes is irrelevant to our problem with the way we see and value ourselves. In a strange sort of way, however unpleasant your boss might be, he or she might actually end up being one of your teachers in the school of life: because they are so difficult, they might actually make you see your value and enrich your life.

⁊⊶⊷

The most common question people ask me is: 'What am I here for?' It might seem a difficult question, but the answer is the same for all of us. It is what I have just explained: we are here because we, as souls, want to grow, to learn more, to progress along our spiritual path – whether we realise this or not.

When people ask me about their life purpose, they are looking for specific answers. We tend to think that if everything is cut and dried for us in life, all our problems will be solved. But when someone asks me, 'What am I here for?', they are actually asking me to restrict their growth as a soul. They hope I will tell them that they're to be a great golfer or healer or actor or whatever, when in fact life provides us with the opportunities to do any one of these things *and* a great deal more.

If we become fixated on only one aspect of our potential, we miss out on the many wider opportunities that will come our way, opportunities that have nothing to do with golf or acting. If we fail to explore these wider opportunities, we are settling for second best in this lifetime. On the other hand, if we open ourselves up to the possibilities, we will experience a life of abundance in the very best sense of the word.

There are lessons for us in everything we do. Perhaps we go into bad relationships over and over again, and continually ask ourselves what we have done to deserve this. Time and time again, we consult our tarot or whatever, but don't get the answers that will allow us to progress, because we are not asking the right questions.

We should be asking: 'What can I learn from these situations? What point am I missing?' We are given many opportunities to grow as we progress through life. But often when we consult our 'props' we do so at a highly emotional time, when the desire for a particular answer is strong, and so the information we receive is distorted.

More than any other, these times we live in are highly charged emotionally. We need to understand that there are real answers for each one of us. Many of the answers are embedded in our memories of the experiences connected to each of our lives – the joys, the sorrows and the triumphs. If we open ourselves to these memories, without fail the knowing will come through to guide us in the right way.

This guidance could be anything from a feeling of relief to a person phoning to send their love. The universe will use anything and everything that is available in this world and in other dimensions to give us the answers and direction we need. We could turn on the television set and see a program that speaks to our need; we might hear a piece of music on radio, or pick up a magazine and read an article that helps us with our problem. All we have to do is to be open to the fact that there is an answer for us. The secret is not to determine how the answer will come to us, but rather to be sure the answer will come.

Too often when we're hurt and feeling lonely, we cut ourselves off from life. We don't go out. We stop listening to the
radio and watching TV. We stop participating in life. We justify
this by saying we've been hurt so we are going to hide away,
but what we are really doing is surrounding ourselves with our
own negativity and fears. Inevitably, when we do this, the
answers we get back are the wrong ones.

When we are dealing with hurtful life experiences, we need
to stand back from our own emotional responses so that we can
see more clearly. Too often we tend to live our lives like the
last act of some great drama, believing that no one has ever
experienced what we are going through. We view life as if it
were an exam we are doomed to fail. We're stuck in yesterday,
so we lose today and sabotage tomorrow; and we miss out on
the joy of simply living on the earth plane.

Especially in difficult times, we need to have the courage to
embrace life and to remind ourselves that we are not being punished by God or the universe. It is simply life's way. We are
here to grow beyond our adversities in order to become the
healthy, happy, prosperous human beings we were created to be.

ॐ

On the relationship front, sadly, we have the idea that each of
us has a soul mate, and that if only we could find that person,
we would live happily ever after. We picture someone who is
exactly like ourselves, who will pre-empt our every thought. But
if we were to attract someone who thinks the same thoughts we
think, who wants to do the same things we want to do, we
wouldn't have any need for anyone else; there would be no
room for growth or wider experiences.

A true soul mate is not a reality on this earth plane. The
perfect half of each of us exists throughout the universe in many
personalities, and being with them makes us feel totally accepted,
understood and complete. The best we can hope to achieve in
this life is to be attracted to a person who enjoys the things we
do, who wants only the best for us and will put us first, and who
we treat in the same way. In other words, we develop a deep
and abiding respect for each other. Then we might come to call

ourselves soul mates. It's a match made on earth, as we work together and grow over the years.

We all belong to spiritual families which allow us to share with many people with whom we find ourselves on the same level of thought and understanding. We meet people in this life who are on the same wavelength, but it is not necessarily a romantic involvement. It might be two friends, a child and a parent, a daughter- and mother-in-law. The important thing to understand is that often these meetings are brief; we find we have to continue our journeys separately. This allows each of us to go on learning. It is no great tragedy, because we will share our time and experiences when we are all back in the spirit world anyway.

⁓

As we come into the womb, we carry deep within us the knowledge that everything is happening according to the divine plan for our soul's happiness and growth. We go through a process of assimilation before we regain a lot of our memories, and sometimes we lose sight of the purpose of our journey. We can get hooked on the 'what ifs' and 'if onlys'. Far too often we may find ourselves reviewing the flaws of our childhood, for example. Forgetting that these were the conditions we chose on returning to earth, we do not recognise them as a part of our growth. Our learning process involves dealing with each unique blend of emotions that is characteristic of this physical world.

7

ℳAKING THE MOST OF OUR TIME ON EARTH

SCIENTISTS HAVE PROVED TIME AND AGAIN that we use only a fraction of our brain and, therefore, only a small part of our potential. Each of us has returned to earth with our own unique gifts and our own soul's growth to attend to.

The more we can get a sense of just how special each and every life is, the more we can grow into our true potential. I'm not a psychic or healer, you say, but that is not entirely true. As we grow spiritually, our intuitive faculties open and more things are revealed to us, including by psychic means.

We all have the ability to heal and often practise forms of healing in daily life without even realising it. One of the laws concerning healing is that we do not help the process if we're fighting it.

Anyone who has had an accident involving a burn will agree that this is a very painful injury. We automatically reach for some soothing agent because it's painful to look at the injury. Panic and fear spread through our mind and body. These emotions may only be momentary, but still they are there as part of the burn. Most people pull away from the injured area. They don't want to look at it, they want to forget it. The constant throbbing, however, keeps them aware of the pain, and pain thoughts keep echoing through the mind. When we become angry with our injury and try to think about something else in order to take our minds off the pain, we are using more mental energy fighting it than it takes to heal the wound.

Children understand this process intuitively. How often have you observed them when they are playing together? One falls over and scrapes his knee; he then gets up and continues to play. When the game finishes, he has forgotten about his injury. Because he was more interested in the game than his accident, he refused to see himself hurt, sore or injured. By giving no energy to the injury, he transcended the pain. His determination to carry on playing has moved his conscious mind from the injury, enabling his inherent healing ability to take over, allowing the subconscious mind to proceed unimpaired by negative thoughts and emotions. This child's injury will heal painlessly and at least three times faster than is considered normal.

Another child falls over, bruising his elbow; he stays on the ground, waiting tearfully for the adults to help him. He is then taken away from the game and his injury is attended to. He won't continue to play because his mind is on his injury. The healing process will take longer and the bruise will continue to cause him pain until it is healed.

A third child falls over after hurting his foot. The parent runs over to him, helps the tearful child to get back on his feet, and examines the injury. The parent tells the child they are alright and can resume playing if they wish. With the parent assuring him he is alright, the child wipes his tears away and continues to play. When he finishes playing, he immediately goes to his parent, wanting more reassurance that his injured foot will be alright.

The third child's injury will heal in what is medically considered the correct amount of time, but he is more prone to complications, such as infection of the wound, because he continually needs reassurance from others that his injury is getting better. His conscious mind is dwelling on how sore the wound is. He's imagining that it looks worse than the last time he examined it. In transmitting his doubts to the wound, he creates certain 'low' areas in his immunity. This slows down the natural healing process and allows the possibility of infection.

We are all children. It's never too late to learn how to apply our own natural healing instincts to whatever ails us.

There is a vast difference between healing, and programming our minds to believe that we haven't got a problem. If an operation is necessary or we are on prescribed medication, let the healing process accelerate our recovery time. When we are in pain and don't know what is wrong with our body, we should consult a physician; once we have a diagnosis and appropriate treatment, we should saturate the diseased area with blue light, at the same time thanking God for our perfect healing. People are often afraid to seek medical help because they think it is better not to know what is wrong. They may instead seek healing, not realising that their fear will stop the healing process until they have acknowledged and confronted it.

We need to review the possibilities and probabilities of those unseen energies and conditions that coexist within us. In doing so, we gain insights that can give us a better understanding of our emotional nature.

The ability to activate healing energy lies within us all. And the opportunities for healing are endless and often unexpected. Every evening at 6 pm, in every Returned Servicemen's League club across Australia, a moment of silence is held. The Ode of Remembrance is recited: 'They shall not grow old as we that are left grow old. Age shall not weary them, nor the years condemn. At the going down of the sun and in the morning, we shall remember them. Lest we forget.'

In that brief moment of stillness, even if only some of the people who are forced to pause actually stop to remember with love those who have passed, the opportunity for healing is enormous. Those who pause with a genuine desire, however humble, to honour the dead – even for the briefest of moments – probably have no idea what they have done in that single instant. They too have joined the wave of healing which flows on to those in need in this life, and to those who have passed over. This healing, for example, touches the multitude of soldiers who have long passed over, and the many departed soldiers whose work is now to help soldiers in need in this life, regardless of their race or the countries they are fighting for.

Why do these soldiers choose to help others, even those who in this life they would have regarded as enemies? Because once in the spirit world, these departed soldiers see that pain and suffering is universal and that we are all one. Thus these soldiers in spirit have a strong desire to help other soldiers in need because they know the terrible realities of war, the dreadful suffering and awful danger.

Whether or not we consider ourselves to be healers is not the point. Understanding the wonder and power of a simple, heartfelt prayer is what matters. Basically, all we need is an earnest desire to help someone in need, and God does the rest. Now when I look back at my own Catholic upbringing, I understand the value of masses for the dead and of lighting a candle for someone who has passed on. Even the simple act of choosing and lighting a candle for someone in need or for someone who has passed over releases a powerful healing energy throughout the universe. Exactly how and where that healing touches is not for us to decide. That is in the hands of God. The important thing is that we have been part of the process by making even the simplest of kind gestures.

＊

Healing is only one area of our hidden potential. Everybody has been on earth before. We all have access to our previous experiences. Frequently, people will pursue interests they have been involved with in former lives. If someone wants to be a doctor, for example, that person probably has a foundation of prior knowledge on which to build. And, again, the more we become in tune with our true selves, the more we are able to access knowledge from former lives.

Another way we access knowledge is when we are asleep. Every single one of us goes somewhere when we sleep. The current concerns that occupy our daily lives dictate where we go when we first fall asleep. If we're very tied up in our career path, for example, that will influence where we journey.

We might be concerned about the future of our workplace and be secretly wondering whether the business is likely to grow in the future. If this is the case, we'll probably travel into the future to see how the business is faring a few years hence. When we get there, we'll note what's going on, who's in charge and who's working there. We might then wake up and remember that we were running down corridors surrounded by strange faces. That's when we will ask what the dream was all about and who the people were. Let's say that a number of years pass and we find we're still with the same organisation. The managing director has just died. For the first time we're meeting the new managing director and, strangely, we feel we've met him before. We then discover we're going to new premises we've never seen before and yet, the place looks familiar – and before we know it, we're talking about deja vu.

Alternatively, we might have a friend or relative on holidays in another country. We want to see how that person is going and so, when we go to sleep that night, our spirit leaves our body. Asleep and out of our physical body, we instantly remember how things work in the astral planes; we only have to think about being with that person to find ourselves there.

How *do* things work on the astral? It's a very simple spiritual principle: like attracts like. It's a universal law that is as true for the spirit world as it is for our world: those of like mind or like energies are drawn together. Thus, beings of all dimensions are frequently drawn together on the astral plane because of their common interests. People who are currently incarnated in this world meet with those who are in spirit. Often these souls formed interest groups many thousands of years ago to share information and to help each other with a particular project through time.

There are, for example, those who are interested in herbal remedies in this life; it would be natural for them to join up with others of the same interests. This gathering and sharing of information plays a very important part in the entry of new inventions and new knowledge to the earth plane. Of course, we are given information that is relevant to our times and to our own specialist knowledge. A herbalist is not going to wake up with a formula for nuclear fission, but rather with a formula for treating a common cold, because this group, in this life and in the spirit world, have been working to come up with a remedy. Always, this work is for the benefit of humankind.

Similarly, healing is happening on the astral all the time. Someone who is ill will receive healing from the astral. Often sick people drifting in and out of consciousness will make the comment that they saw someone they know while in that unconscious state. They put this experience down to imagination or drugs, when in fact it's an astral experience.

Recently I was feeling unwell and woke about 3 am to see my friend and acupuncturist, Diane McKeon, standing beside the bed. I was out of my body at the time and could see her working on me, giving me healing. Then, before she left, she gave me strict instructions to get some calcium, telling me sternly to get out of bed and write down what she'd said. I did as I was told before heading off to sleep again. I rang Diane the next morning and thanked her for the overnight healing, then repeated her instructions to me, saying, 'But you needn't think I'm going to pay you for after-hours house calls!'

All that is necessary when going to sleep is the desire to help others and you will do so. You might simply have the desire to do something worthwhile to help the environment. That's enough – you don't have to be specific about what exactly this task should be. The desire alone will give you the vibration to visit like minds who are doing that very same work. Personally, I feel the best approach is simply to ask for guidance about what you should be doing.

There are always the lighter moments to being out in the astral. I was having a week's holiday in the country with my girlfriends and our friend Kosti. We had all been playing a card game, Phase Ten, in the lounge room before going to bed. Kosti had never played cards before, so we decided to teach him how to play.

On retiring, everybody went to their respective bedrooms, except for Kosti, who ended up sleeping on the sofa. I got up in the middle of the night for a drink and, sneaking past him, was startled when he sat bolt upright and said, 'Is that the real you, Margaret?'

I replied that it was me and asked Kosti why he had asked.

'Because I've been playing cards with you and all your relatives in the astral, so I didn't know whether I was awake or whether we were both still on the astral,' was his reply.

I laughed. I knew exactly which of my relatives he was talking about and just how disgusted they'd be that we were playing what they would consider to be a kids' game. I had some mad keen card players in the family, to say the least! They'd obviously decided to take matters into their own experienced hands and had been giving Kosti lessons in proper card playing.

Always, in everything we do, we have the opportunity to learn. Part of this process is gaining access to good information. That's where our discernment comes in. I am often overwhelmed by the realisation of how much more I need to learn. I have no magic keys to unlock the doors of spiritual mysteries, but what I do know is that people fear what they don't understand. Education eliminates the fear. Part of what we come to understand is that we are spirit in a body here and now, and that we never die.

Each of us is unique. We each have our own ways of dealing with events in our lives. So when we are searching for the lessons from life events, we must first ask: 'Is my way of handling the situation helping me to progress?' If we can't assess this ourselves, we need to read or hear about the experiences of others and see how they have handled similar situations. Then we will find a way through. We may realise, for example, that we are feeling sorry for ourselves and then be able to look at the circumstances clearly and objectively.

What we have to aim for is 'at-onement' with our higher self. This means we need to spend time getting to know and understand ourselves. We should use whatever tools we can to look at ourselves in a fair and balanced way. If we do this sincerely, calmly and in an unbiased fashion that is not fearful, we are open to receive and are moving towards at-onement.

Often, though, when we ask, we do not correctly interpret what we are shown. We might ask if we are going to marry a person we are seeing and like. For a brief second, we glimpse another person who looks quite different, and our emotional nature dismisses the message. It is not what we expected or hoped for, so we dismiss it. What we should be saying is, 'If this is a true message from my higher self, even though I don't want this to be the answer, I will be still. I will let time pass and wait to see the outcome of this situation.' What will no doubt happen is that the current relationship will crumble. In time, we will meet and end up settling with the person we glimpsed months or years previously.

Whether we realise it or not, each of us has contacted our higher self many times. Every time we go through the process of asking a question, receiving an answer and acknowledging the information, we get better at it. We begin to separate the erratic voice of our emotions from the calming voice of our higher self, and to hear the messages clearly.

The more we listen, the stronger the link grows, until one day it becomes an instantaneous and profound knowing, infusing the whole of our being. We become deeply and profoundly aware that we are being taken care of and that we will triumph, no matter how bad the situation appears to be. Often we do not reach this place until we have exhausted all other possible avenues and stopped the process of arguing with ourselves. Then we are left with nowhere to go except to still our minds and listen to what the universe has been trying to tell us.

Recently I had an unnerving experience when a dear friend, Dave, was rushed to hospital with a suspected heart attack. For three days and nights, I assured the family that although this wasn't going to be pleasant, he would be fine and that this was a minor problem. Dave was transferred to a hospital close to where I live and where I have friends on the medical staff. I visited him the first night of his transfer, and he was bright and happy and waiting to have an angiogram the following morning.

Early the next day, however, I received a call from one of my friends at the hospital to tell me Dave was unconscious, having had a massive heart attack during the angiogram. He asked me to phone Dave's wife, which I did. Then I went into shock. I could not understand why my messages about Dave's illness had been so wrong.

Over the next fifteen minutes, however, everything became clear. It transpired that a mistake had been made. It was not Dave who was seriously ill, but another patient. Dave's angiogram showed no serious heart problems.

When I had time later, I reviewed the situation calmly. My emotions had not only overridden my higher self, but had also shut out the voices of my spirit friends – all my normal sources of help, the sources I use every single day in my work. Had I been giving this information as part of a reading for somebody else, I would have been able to see things clearly.

We must always be careful not to allow ourselves to be carried away with the moment. Of course, we are emotional beings – that's what makes us human – but we need to stay balanced. Remember, our higher self is non-emotional. It can see beyond the everyday emotions and concerns. In accessing our higher self, we are able to access knowledge and experience gained over lifetimes.

$\mathscr{T}$HE APPROACH OF DEATH

EVEN WITH THE KNOWLEDGE OF THE LANDSCAPE of death, the approach of the death of a loved one is painful. No matter how far down the path we go on our journey towards enlightenment, we are still bound to feel sorrow as someone we love begins to slip away from us.

Before I move on to speak of the process of dying, of death and of life in the world of spirit, I want to touch on the topic of Alzheimer's disease. It affects a great many people we know today, partly because of the quantity of chemicals we are now ingesting with our modern lifestyles.

Let me tell you Annelie's story. Annelie is one of my closest and dearest friends. We have worked together for many years, doing public readings, teaching classes and giving lectures. She sits next to me with her sketching pad, pastels and crayons, and as I tune into the spirit world, so does she. While I am giving messages to people from their deceased loved ones, she produces likenesses of these people in the spirit world for their loved ones in this world to see.

When I am teaching and lecturing, she will sketch the students' guides.

Annelie was a student in my psychic and spiritual development classes when her mother, Elizabeth, was diagnosed with Alzheimer's disease. This gave me the opportunity to observe the changes, as they happened, to Elizabeth's mind – how the disease affected her psychic abilities, spiritual knowledge and normal personality.

Her memory started to be affected in much the same way as those of us not in the early stages of Alzheimer's disease, but the difference I noticed at that time was that when she forgot something, she was unable to retrieve the memory. We can all forget what we went into a particular room for, but if we retrace our steps, we can usually recall what it was. If not, we can be certain that before the day ends, something in our memory will be triggered and we will remember what it was that we were intending to do.

Elizabeth was a wonderful cook. When we had functions or parties, she always cooked her special cheesecake, one for me and one for the function. So it was a great loss to her family and friends when she had to stop. At first she forgot her recipes. Then she started to forget to turn the stove off, causing her to burn her hands and her arms. If she forgot that she had something on the stove or in the oven, small fires would break out. Finally, she forgot to eat.

Medically, the sufferers of this disease are said to be going through a breakdown of the neural pathways in the brain, causing short-term memory loss and disorientation in relation to their surroundings and the people around them. Eventually the sufferer is unable to remember their family or friends. The brain is like a motor that runs the physical body; if it short-circuits, it can still function but it has lost the use of an important part.

The motor that runs the spiritual body is not reliant on the same materials from which the physical body is made: blood, flesh, bones and tissue. The motor that runs the spiritual body is indestructible. It is the essence of all living creatures. It is a spark given from the creator.

Imagine a very brilliant light, embodying every conceivable colour. It looks like a fire burning and mastering all things. Its size is so enormous that it fills all the universe. It can never be seen by the human eye. If one tiny spark were to touch the human body, the body would disintegrate. A fire that burns throughout eternity, unlike the fire we are familiar with, it can never be put out or contained. All of humanity bathes in its light.

Every day God sends a token to remind us of the creator's existence. It is a tiny spark taken from the whole and similar to the one within us that we call the soul. The visual reminder he sends for all to see is the sun: our sun, like our creator, the brilliance of which is likened to the ever-burning, warming, life-giving, nurturing universal fire – the creator of all.

As sons and daughters of our creator, we carry within us a spark of the divine and, like our creator, we come in various disguises. For the purpose of being born of the flesh into a world of matter, we have been given a physical body to travel through this world so that we can grow through our experiences.

As Elizabeth's illness progressed, her husband, parents and friends who were in the spirit world became her constant companions, intervening to help her through this dreadful period of her life. They would often put thoughts in her mind to check the stove, to see if she'd locked the door and so on. When she became frustrated and agitated, I could see them giving her healing and calming her.

As her condition deteriorated, it was very difficult for them to use this process and they would concentrate on one of the grandchildren or daughters to get them to phone her or visit. Perhaps those individuals had recently talked to her and had no reason to phone, but of course they would follow the thought, often thinking it was their own mind, only to find that they were very much needed on those occasions. Eventually, Elizabeth had to be admitted to a nursing home.

I would often talk to her at night when her body was sleeping and her spirit would astral travel. Temporarily freed from her physical body, Elizabeth did not have a problem with her brain or her personality. She was the same person she had always been before her illness. She told me that when she was awake in her physical body, it was like living in a dream state after a repetitive bad dream.

The people who were part of her everyday earthly existence

appeared unreal, often blanketed in a fog as if she were surrounded by strangers. Every now and then a beloved face would emerge from that fog like a haze, and it would be a daughter or a grandchild or a friend. But those times became more infrequent. The people in the spirit world were not clouded and hazy; they appeared more real to her than the people from the world she was living in.

At times she would be aware of the fog lifting. She wasn't sure what triggered this: sometimes a loved one having a conversation with her when she found herself quite lucid and able to join in, at other times a familiar action or word. When things started to cloud or fog over again, she would be compelled to run to get out, unable to see her spirit people. Panic would take over because the fear of being cut off from both worlds was more than she could bear. Then things would calm down, and once more she could see her spirit friends.

Her spiritual experiences became more frequent. It was as if she was watching her physical self, while unable to communicate with her earthly loved ones visiting her in the nursing home.

I was with her when she died, and I officiated at her funeral. When I was writing her service, she helped me from the spirit world, telling me what she wanted to say to those she had left behind.

I miss her physical presence, but I can't grieve for her. Every time I think of her, I remember her absolute joy at leaving her physical body for the last time, and being held in her husband's arms.

At the funeral she was there with all her family and friends from the spirit world. She looked younger, vibrant and alive.

If you have a loved one with Alzheimer's, try this exercise. It's important to be in a calm, relaxed state of mind. If you are visiting, it's important that the patient is sleeping, as this makes it easier to access the subconscious mind and spiritual self. You can use this process from your home; distance and time are never a problem. Imagine a beautiful blue shimmering light filling the space you are occupying. Immerse yourself and the patient in that light. Keep visualising the colour and use it to quieten your breathing and to relax as much as possible. Say a short prayer or words stating your need for help and guidance from people in the spirit world.

Don't worry if you have never known anyone who has died; we all have deceased great-grandparents, aunts, uncles and so on. Ask for help – you will be pleasantly surprised. When you start this process, keep it simple. Don't expect to have a full conversation in the early stages; it takes time, practice and patience. Fifteen minutes is enough at first; you are learning to use your mind to communicate, so begin with just a few words. 'I love you' is always a good start. When you become more proficient, you can say all the things you want to say.

If you are living with an Alzheimer's sufferer, you will feel a lot of anxiety, guilt and grief throughout your day. Don't let these emotions build up. Use the process I have given you to deal with them each night. It's simple and very effective. Don't be afraid to talk about your feelings when you are communicating.

We are not saints. We do lose our tempers, and life can be very unfair at times. Say it! Release it, and know how to forgive yourself. Remember, love is always there and you are never alone.

When you finish, always say thank you to God. This acknowledgment helps to close you off; otherwise, you are sensitive and open to negative factors. Those spirit friends and healers who are helping you have been given the signal to finish communicating until you desire it again.

Senility is the weakness of mental infirmity of old age. We are all aware of senility as a basic concept, but what does it really mean? There is no doubt that there is a medical condition called senility. My experience in dealing with people supposedly senile, however, is vastly different from what is generally accepted. I see much in common with children said to be psychic and aged people said to be senile. The imagination, in conjunction with the normal senses, is an integral part of our physical nature.

The child will see spirit people and animals because they are no different in form and shape to anyone in a physical body.

When something is normal, people don't draw attention to it, so neither do children until they realise they are able to see things adults can't.

For the aged person, it's the same thing. They've lost the clear boundary between this world and the spirit world. They can't distinguish time. When they talk, the people around them can't relate. We are housed within our auric field, which contains all experiences from the moment we arrive. So when the aged person opens up psychically, they see (for example) Aunt Mary, who was a real, long-term part of their life while they were growing up. Memories then flood in of experiences around Aunt Mary – other members of the family, the house, the pastimes. The aged person becomes lost in the reality of that moment, reliving the furniture, the tiny details.

Children, on the other hand, don't have the subconscious memory because they've just arrived on earth. So they connect directly with the world of pure spirit, the world that is most familiar to them, since that is where they've just come from.

When we spend time with a person who is mentally and emo-tionally preparing for the journey into the spirit realms (dying), the normal activity of the conscious and subconscious mind alters, causing a shift in that person's perceptions. Basically it creates a distortion of the real distinction, as we understand it, between this world and the spirit world.

If we take the concept of time, for instance, we will find that the aged person's concept of time has shifted from the way we normally view it. Suddenly, for them there are no boundaries to the past, present and future. Events relating to the long dead, places left behind, houses, countries, conversations with dead loved ones all take place in the room where their physical body is.

When we are in a physical body, higher knowledge is part of our spiritual make-up but remains separate to the physical part of us, unless we make the effort to reach out for understanding. An aged person who is 'senile' is, in fact, making this transition in preparation for moving on to the spirit world again.

And now to the approach of death. When we reach this stage with a loved one, there is so much to come to terms with, from our own emotional responses of fear, anger and despair to dealing with the fact that this person is going to die, while facing the uncertainty about exactly when this will take place.

In addition to this, there are often circumstances surrounding these departed loved ones that we don't quite understand.

When people are terminally ill or when old age is simply ending their earthly existence, the caregivers may think the dying are experiencing hallucinations caused by the medication or perhaps by senility. In fact, the dying person's perceptions are true; it is the onlookers' reality that is confined to the bricks and mortar of this world called earth.

It is difficult for us to believe at first that the ninety-year-old's dead mother is comforting her, or that the long-dead partner is telling the spouse not to be afraid. It is much easier for us to believe we're hearing the ramblings of a sick person. The fact is that what we're hearing is their communication with a different level of reality.

We also hear stories of a dying person talking of hearing celestial music. There are also numerous accounts of the dying seeing brilliant colours. Often they will talk of a deceased loved one standing by, waiting to take them into the world of spirit. And even when the dying person is too sick to talk, friends and relatives speak of how at their last breath the loved one's face was transformed with a radiant smile. These stories aren't new; they're as old as the spoken word.

If an aged person is dying with a minimal amount of trauma to the physical body, the process is made simple because the person has already become attuned to the other side during the last few months of their life. At this special time, their psychic faculties have opened up and prepared them for their journey.

Not always do our departed loved ones get noticeably sick before they die. And often it's only when we look back that it appears as if at some level they knew they were going to go.

I'm often asked if there are signs and omens that will warn us of death. Certainly, a lot has also been written about different portents of the death of someone close. The fact is that we all create our own reality. If a whole group of people has a set of beliefs which include specific signs that they read as warnings of an impending death, then the group energy of these people will make it so, and it will happen. In some cultures, for example, the sighting or hearing of certain types of owl is a warning of an impending death. However, if we don't belong to the cultures that hold those beliefs, coming across or hearing that same species of owl is unlikely to mean anything other than that we've seen an owl.

This doesn't mean these signs aren't valid or that there aren't ever signals that a person is likely to move on. What is much more common for most of us is that, in the weeks leading up to the death of a loved one, a pattern emerges. However, it is often not until the loved one has passed on that we become aware of what was happening.

A common occurrence preceding a healthy person's passing is that the person has an urgent need to get their life in order. They start tidying up their home, their garage, throwing out items they have accumulated over the years, or perhaps giving treasured trinkets to friends and relatives. They might also clean the windows, drapes and carpets as if they are expecting some occasion when their home is going to be open for inspection.

When questioned about this behaviour, they often reply, 'I just felt like tidying up, it's time I fixed up those things. They've been on my mind, worrying me.'

Then, when everything is in order, the person suddenly dies.

People are shocked and ask, 'Did she know she was going to die? And if she did, how did she know?'

The answer is that the person did in fact know they were about to die, but not necessarily on a conscious level. Their subconscious receives this information long before any event happens. I have found that up to six weeks before a person dies, there is an awareness of their impending departure, often called a premonition. The message can come by way of a dream, a visitation from a deceased person, feelings of dread, or a strong desire to settle old arguments, to tie up loose ends in the work-place, to take that holiday there never seemed to be enough time or money for. This premonition takes many forms, depending on the nature of the person and what particular things are important to them. We're not talking about a clear message – just feelings, anticipation, excitement about getting on with things that are high on the person's priority list.

Often at this time the person will appear confused, anxious, angry and even fearful. The unfortunate thing about these negative emotions is that frequently they end up causing arguments with loved ones or others close to that person. Then the person in question dies and those left behind are full of guilt because of the friction that occurred before the person passed away.

If only these friends and relatives could see and talk to the person now residing in the spirit world, they would feel quite differently. They would see that because of the ability now to understand the wider picture, the deceased person is equally sorry about the friction, wanting friends and relatives to put these incidents behind them so that everyone can get on with their lives.

When people are psychic and correctly trained, they can interpret what is happening and explain it to those on the earth plane. This establishes a healing energy and can eliminate confusion for all concerned. A trained psychic is able to tell the person who is having disturbing dreams whether the cause is psychic or a fear of something occurring because of an upset in their everyday life. In cases where the person is suffering some type of psychological trauma, the psychic would suggest that they see a trained practitioner, such as a psychologist or psychiatrist.

Where dreams are telling of that person's death, the psychic would be working on healing and calming the person's physical body. In such cases the patient would not necessarily know that they were receiving healing from the psychic practitioner because the healing continues long after they have had a reading. They leave the consultation greatly uplifted and reassured that there is nothing ahead that they cannot handle.

If someone from a deceased person's family consults a medium, information can be given that helps put the family members' minds at ease. This is what we call survival evidence.

9

$\mathcal{P}$ASSING OVER INTO SPIRIT

OUR HEARTS GO OUT TO ANYONE we know who is in the process of losing a loved one. When our turn comes to experience this loss, it's often hard to know what to do – the sense of impending loss is so enormous. It's like being lost in a fog, not knowing which way to go.

Even though the dying person might be unconscious, if we have a real need to talk with them, we can still do so either physically or mentally. When the departing person draws close to death, the information from the higher self is accessed through the subconscious mind and then makes its way to the conscious mind. When someone is in a mild or deep coma, the same process applies.

By this stage, the dying person is more in contact with the spirit world than with the physical world. Whatever you communicate by words or thoughts while the dying are in this state goes into their subconscious mind, where they receive it. They can also access this information at a future date; once in spirit, they can access far more than we can on earth. The process of obtaining and absorbing information is much more speedy, and there are fewer distractions.

So, as difficult as it is, if we can channel our energy and grief into calming ourselves and stilling our minds when we're with the loved one, it can make a big difference for us and the person departing. It's so important for the dying to be given as much peace as possible. Our distress only heightens their attachment to this world, making the parting even more difficult than it need be.

Once we have calmed down, we simply wait and listen to our inner voice; we will be impressed in some way as to the right course of action. It might come through a feeling, through an unexpected circumstance or through something the patients themselves suggest. Guidance is always there if we can but still ourselves and listen.

Naturally when we're with people who are very ill, our desire is often for a miracle that will enable them to get better. When, however, we pray for healing in this situation, we have to realise that we do not know what is best for them in terms of the ongoing journey of their soul.

Accepting guidance from our own inner voice is essential because we tend to put judgments on healing and might feel that if a person dies the healing has been wasted. This just isn't the case. The marvellous thing about this healing energy is that it is never wasted. Its benefits are tenfold. Around death it helps those in spirit to assist the dying with their spiritual transition, and especially in that final transition from the physical world to the world of the spirit.

Often when loved ones are passing there's a feeling of help-lessness, but we are all able to help them in their passing. Even though the loved one might no longer be conscious, visualise a blue light in your mind's eye. Immerse the patient in this blue light. Then talk about or think of all those who have gone before whom this person knows or loves. You might not know what they look like – that's not important; knowing their name or the relationship the departed ones have to the dying person is enough. Then, simply ask for the departed to come closer. This helps strengthen the energy between those in the spirit world and those who are passing.

So, no matter how distressed and anguished we are feeling, we are not helpless. By centring on the simple exercise of visualising the blue light, we not only touch the patient but allow the healing energy to flow back to us and everyone present.

At no time are we making the decision between the life and death of this individual. We are simply asking to be of service. This service might well be a healing or the process of transition as in death. Part of the service of those in the spirit world can be the assistance in healing of those in this life. This doesn't necessarily mean that people in spirit have been healers in their former life, but rather that this is a job they've elected to do since they passed over. The opportunities for our growth as souls never ceases.

How does all this work? Well, healing helps to quieten the conscious mind and numb the person's physical pain, enabling spirit friends to access the dying person. This way, spirit friends can help the dying person on their journey into the spirit world. The healing energy also gives the dying comfort by providing them with the same sense of nurture and security they feel when they think of their familiar physical world. This in turn assists them in their progression into spirit. In short, healing energy can give the dying person feelings of pure joy – the peace that passes all understanding. For spirit friends to be able to do their work easily, they need to access the dying person's energy field to calm, reassure and guide them.

There is nothing to be afraid of in helping in this process. Sadly, there is a lot of superstition around death and it has created a great deal of fear. The basic fact is that the dead have no power to call you across to death. They do not have the power of life and death.

The wonder of healing energy is this: the very same healing power that was used to calm the dying person then continues on and flows back to touch all those connected with that person's life. This is what is meant by healing energy being tenfold. It reaches out to all those needing solace, regardless of who they are or where in the world they live. What's more, this energy touches people in different ways, in ways that are appropriate to each. It might simply be a general sense of comfort or a religious renewal, a strengthening of faith. How the healing manifests is unimportant. The important thing is that the healing is there for everybody. Energy is never lost.

As soon as the dying have passed over to the spirit world and seen the people they thought they'd lost in death, they receive immense comfort. At this point, most people's perceptions are heightened in their new surroundings. Without the restrictions of the earth plane, they are free to see things more clearly, to understand things much better.

Accepting guidance is also important, because sometimes our presence is a comfort in the last moments of someone's life – and sometimes it isn't. I can remember when my mum's father developed lung cancer. He died when I was twenty-six. His name was James and he was born in Tipperary, Ireland. He emigrated, met and married my grandmother and they had one daughter, my mum, who in turn had me, the eldest, and my brother Michael. My mum and her father were very close.

When I was eleven months old, I began calling my grandfather Bo-Bo. The family adopted this name, and he was known as Bo-Bo until he died. Bo-Bo had a brother by the name of Jack, who had died of an asthma attack before I was born. My mum was also a chronic asthmatic, so emergency trips to the hospital were a normal part of my life.

I cannot remember a time when my grandfather wasn't there for my mum. He was always in the emergency room at the hospital, waiting all night, until Mum was out of danger. He doted on my brother and myself, and not a week would pass without time spent with him and my grandmother. He was a kind-hearted, good-humoured man, but very straight-laced. No one ever argued with him; when he said something, you did it. He never smacked us; he didn't raise his voice. The tone was enough to pull us into line.

When I was thirteen, I began to realise how stubborn my beloved Bo-Bo was. I started to argue with him, and the family would speculate as to how long the ensuing silences would last between us. Who was going to give in first? They thought these situations very funny, because I was equally stubborn. At the time, I didn't think it funny at all.

We were a Catholic family, and my grandfather gave much of his time to the church. He was a painter by trade, and so he was always painting one church or another. When I would give him messages from his dead brother, Jack, he was delighted. He would ask about his mother and other relatives whom I had never met. In this way, I was able to experience, at an early age, a wonderful camaraderie with his family.

He didn't understand how I did it any more than I did. It wasn't as though I sat around all the time giving messages from the spirit world. I was too busy, to quote my grandfather, 'being a tomboy, always out playing'.

He was admitted to hospital the week that he died. I would visit him each day, and I was with him on the afternoon of the day he passed over. On that final afternoon, I was sitting talking to him when suddenly the room was filled with the most beautiful light. There was a hazy effect of clouded white light and I could see spirit people, some of whom I recognised as relatives to whom I had previously spoken. Others I didn't know. As I held his hand, he drifted from consciousness to semi-consciousness.

As his spirit left his physical body, his vital signs were of a person in an unconscious state, and yet I was privileged to be able to hear everything that was happening to him. His mother and father were holding him and telling him not to be afraid, telling him that he would be out of pain soon and that they would all be together.

His brother Jack was there, too. As they chatted excitedly to one another, a nurse walked into Bo-Bo's hospital room and touched his body to take his blood pressure. The spirit body jolted back into his physical body. His eyes flew open, and it was obvious that he was very confused. When the nurse left, I asked him what his mother and father had said to him.

He replied that he didn't remember and wanted to know how I knew about his dream. As I tried to explain what was happening to him, he became upset and said he was afraid he was losing his mind. I began to reassure him he wasn't, and then he drifted back into his semi-conscious state.

My mum and my grandmother had recently left the hospital

after being with Bo-Bo all morning. The priest arrived to give him the last rites of the Catholic church, and I left the room to telephone my mum and my grandmother. When I returned, the priest had not finished and I walked into one of the most beautiful scenes I have ever witnessed, and one that I will never forget. The priest was praying. He was surrounded by a bright, golden haze. Spirit people were standing and kneeling, all praying with the priest. There were nuns reciting the Hail Mary as they fingered rosary beads. A choir was singing.

It was as if I had walked into a church, but the singing that filled the air was unlike any heard here on earth. Words can never do justice to such magnificence. The tears streamed down my face as the priest tried to console me. I could not explain that my tears were of joy and not sadness. I had just been privileged to witness something so wonderful. My grandfather was at one with God and his religious beliefs were eliminating his fears and restoring his faith.

Once again, his eyes opened. I was surprised, as I thought I had just witnessed his passing. Mentally, I prayed and asked, 'How can I help him? What can I do to make it easier?' I then started projecting my thoughts to his spirit self, telling him to let go and not be afraid.

Suddenly, he sat bolt upright in his bed and pulled his hand out of mine. I had never seen him so angry, his beautiful blue eyes more vibrant, more full of life than I had ever seen them before. He looked at me accusingly, 'You're trying to kill me! Wild horses can't make me leave here and neither can you. Get out and leave me alone.'

I was in shock and had to leave the room. I sat down outside his room, bewildered, angry – and then amused. I kept hearing his statement about the wild horses. I had never heard him say that before. Then I became aware of a familiar spirit presence. She was one of my teachers.

'Don't worry,' she said, 'he didn't mean it. He's a stubborn man, very strong-willed.' How many times had I heard that one over the years? 'If you want to help him die, you must go home,' she went on.

I was horrified at the thought of leaving him.

She explained, 'While you are with him, he will keep fighting to hold on to life. Even when he's unconscious, he senses your presence. It's everything he loves and holds dear. It makes it difficult for his loved ones in spirit to help him. He will fight his physical pain instead of giving in and letting go, thus causing unnecessary mental and emotional anguish.'

I asked if he would have the same problems with the rest of the family and she assured me he would. I impressed on her that I wanted to be with my grandfather when he passed over.

'You can do that from your home,' she said. 'When it's time, you can watch what is happening. We will send a guide to help you.'

When the family arrived I told my mum what had happened. They kissed Grandfather goodbye and we went home.

Two hours later, my brother Michael, who had died less than two years previously, came to me and it was as my teacher had promised. I went with Michael in my spirit body and was able to observe everything that happened to my grandfather as he made the transition from this world to the next.

The memories of that experience are so vivid they'll be etched in my mind forever. When Michael left me to join Bo-Bo, Grandfather threw his arms around the grandson he thought he'd lost and cried like a baby. I became upset and immediately found myself back in my body.

I have sat with countless people as they make their transition from this world to the next. And regardless of the person's religious beliefs (or lack of them), I have witnessed similar scenes. In my work as a medium, seeing-through the eyes and memories of those in spirit as they give survival evidence to their loved ones, again and again I have witnessed the moment of transition from this world to the next. Whether the passing was through natural death, through the murder of a child or adult, or through suicide, not once has anyone crossed into the spirit world without someone being there to comfort them.

This is the true meaning of the 'brotherhood of man'. Just as, in this world, people join together to help the victims of a catastrophe, so in the spirit world is it common practice to help those in need. Comforting those who have newly arrived is an experience of great joy to those already in spirit.

10

$\mathscr{B}$ACK HOME IN THE WORLD OF SPIRIT

WHEN THEY HAVE JUST LOST A LOVED ONE, people will often recount feeling a great coldness around them, a kind of coldness they've never experienced before. What's happening is that the auras of the living and the deceased person are coming into contact as the deceased person is departing. At this point, the deceased person's aura is no longer a part of the energy we all live in. But there is a short transition period before their aura is sufficiently energised to enable them to move about freely in their spirit body. During this brief period, the deceased person's aura gives off a cold and dark vibration. There's nothing sinister about this. The person has simply shed the denser energies of earth and is gearing up for the much finer energy of the spirit world. Years ago I worked in a butcher's shop and was in and out of the cold storage room; I remember thinking that this was the closest I'd come to that feeling of extreme cold around the newly deceased.

A great deal has been spoken and written about how long the spirit does or does not stay around after the body is clinically dead. Basically, this depends on the deceased person's religious beliefs, on their personality and on the conditions they've left behind.

A family man with two young children who is killed on the way home from work is going to be in a state of shock and concern. His first thoughts on discovering he is dead are to find his wife and let her know he has survived this transition we call death. He will be upset at his predicament.

This is very different from the person who has been dying painfully and slowly for months from an incurable disease. This person has had a great deal of time to come to terms with the knowledge that they're dying. For them, the absolute relief of leaving this life is major because they are instantly whole and out of pain.

Tyrannical people, who cannot stand to think of life going on without their permission, are a different story again. Spiritual laws are set in motion to protect us from this type of personality and to protect their loved ones from their interference once they are in spirit. These people are denied access to their family until they see the error of their ways. Before they can gain access, their motivation has to be of pure origin: of love and consideration, and genuine concern for their loved ones. Again, I must stress that there is nothing to fear from the dead.

When people die, the biggest shock they experience is not the actual death; it's the fact that they find themselves not dead, but alive. Very quickly, they learn basic differences between the world just left and the one just entered. Regardless of the cause of death, whether it be through age, violent means, long illness or an accident, there is always someone there to guide people to the dimension of light and love. This could be a relative, a friend or a spirit guide or teacher.

They start to feel subtle but definite differences in their new spirit body, although it usually appears to be exactly the same as the one with which they travelled through their earthly existence. If a person had a limb amputated in life, however, this is not evident in spirit because the spirit body is whole. In fact, it's the aura. Nothing can damage the spirit body that is encased in the physical body within its own energy field.

There is no immediate change in the thinking process of the person who has just died, and the personality will always remain the same. That is the part of our nature that makes us unique and sets us apart. Those memories and experiences that were foremost in the mind at the time of passing are still there, but are quickly becoming a memory. They are now being replaced by the current experiences, which prove our continuing existence. This is why the biggest shock is not the death, but the realisation that we are immortal.

When we first go into the spirit world, we tend to be preoccupied with our own anguish and concerns. But this stage passes, and we start to think and care about others. We can see and feel the pain of others and so we become more compassionate; as we have said earlier, regardless of whether we're in the physical or the spirit world, we never stop learning. In time, and depending on our personalities, many of our prejudices and misunderstandings dissipate once we are in the spirit world. Many of us outgrow our personal problems and see things more clearly.

When we are in spirit, we are in a position to see how the healing energies work in the animal, vegetable and human world. This understanding is intuitive, just as the newborn baby quickly understands that nourishment comes through breast milk. Spiritual knowledge comes to us as second nature when we're in the spirit world.

People are always asking me what it's like in the spirit world. Rather than my telling you, here's Paula's story.

Paula grew up in a country town and, at eighteen, was away from home for the first time. She had started university and was driving home for a short holiday when she had a car accident and died.

Paula had always wanted to be a journalist. She was an only child and had had a good life with no tragedy, so she had little baggage when she passed over. And as it hadn't been that long since she'd left her home in the spirit world, Paula quickly readjusted. She decided to tell her story from the other side. Here it is.

꙰

I opened my eyes and Mum was sitting beside me, holding my hand. My dad was standing next to her.

'What happened? Where am I?'

They told me that I had been in a car accident and I was in intensive care in our local hospital. The room started to fade; their faces and voices seemed to be coming from a distance. The last thing I remember was Mum crying and telling me she loved me.

A few days before this, I had had a conversation with a school friend about death and what happens to us when we die. She believed that we joined up with our relatives and friends who had already died. I said I hadn't thought about it, I was so busy worrying about life. And because there had been no deaths in my family, if there was a spirit world I wouldn't know anyone there anyway.

The hospital room is gone. I am being propelled through a shaft of brilliant white light. It has the appearance of a tunnel. I'm caught up in some kind of flow of energy and it is pushing me towards a group of beings bathed in different coloured lights. As I draw closer to them, I realise that they are people and without those lights emanating from them, they look the same as normal people on earth.

I know I have never seen them before, but there is a feeling of comfort and love and familiarity. I feel a sense of realisation, as if thoughts are telling me things but I'm not certain what it is that I am being told. I only know everything is as it should be. I know I am dead; my whole being is full of this awareness. Yet I don't feel any different. It's as if I always knew it was like this.

A lady separates from the others. She steps forward and reaches out to me. She is putting her arms around me. There is something about her, there's a feeling that I get when my mum or grandmother hugs me. She is welcoming me and she tells me not to be afraid. The love I feel from her is overwhelming. I know it's not Mum, but there's so much about her that reminds me of my mum, and I feel safe.

'My name is Edna,' she says. 'I am your great-grandmother. Your mother is my grand-daughter, and this is Arthur, your great-grandfather.'

Then she introduces me to my great-aunts, uncles and various assortment of other relatives. 'And here are all your relatives from your father's side of the family,' she explains.

I am finding that I don't have my usual feelings of awkwardness when meeting people for the first time. It's as if I have known them all of my life. They are so genuinely pleased to see me. There is an instant belonging as if I'm at one with all of them and always have been.

'Edna, I want to tell Mum and Dad and my grandparents that I am alright and that I'm not alone. I want to let them know that I am with all of you. Will you take me back through that tunnel so that I can tell them?'

'I'm sorry, darling, it's impossible to use that particular way. There is a point in the tunnel when the vibrations change to the refined spirit world. People often find themselves stopped there when they have near death experiences. I will tell you a story about a friend of mine who is in the spirit world. It will explain the tunnel better than I can.

'My friend's name is Miriam. One day she was visited by the most beautiful being I have ever seen. If I were alive on earth and saw him, I would have been so sure that God had appeared and spoken to me. His presence was felt by everyone here. We could listen as he communicated with Miriam. His thoughts were like music and their sound seemed to heighten every sense in your mind and body, causing us all to be tuned in to him. He radiated an energy of pure love that healed and uplifted us. Speculation swept through the crowd about his origin and how we should address him. Was he a saint, a holy man or an angel?

''I come from the same place you have,'' he said. ''I have lived in the same worlds that you have; I have journeyed a little farther on my path than you have. The world I live in is the one you will inhabit. I am neither saint nor holy man and I could never be an angel. Please call me friend. We are all messengers of the Creator and by my presence, I teach. Everyone is a teacher. But only those teachers who understand the truth radiate that unique light that touches the soul, enabling the spirit to be uplifted from the pain of ignorance and the darkness of despair.''

'He then addressed Miriam, and we were all able to hear him. "Your youngest grand-daughter has just had an accident on earth. Her spirit has been prematurely propelled from her physical body. She is hovering above her body watching the hospital staff trying to resuscitate her. It does not have to be the end of her earthly journey.

' "As her spirit leaves that hospital and makes its way into the light, there is a special place we can meet her. But if she passes that point, she no longer has a choice. The life force will permanently leave her physical body and she will continue on to this dimension. She knows and loves you. When she sees you, the joy that she feels will help me to use that vibration to talk to her and explain the spiritual implication of her existence. This will uplift her and help her in making a decision whether or not to go back to earth.

' "I am here to guide you to that special place in the tunnel. It is impossible to reach the earth dimension from here using the tunnel. Its energy is of such a nature as to assist the spirit in making that transition known as death. The light in the tunnel is pure energy that vibrates in one direction only — even when the person is stopped and decides to go back to earth or is told to go back, they do not travel back to their body the same way they came. Often they will feel the same rush of energy pulling them back, but it's in the direction of earth. When they wake up, they are back in their body. Unlike the vivid memories of their experience coming to the tunnel, they have no memories of how they travelled back."

'Miriam asked him if her grand-daughter would be safe as she made her journey to the tunnel.

'He answered, "There is only one force, one energy. It manifests as pure light and it draws you forever upwards, taking on the appearance of a tunnel. The force is God's love for all creatures — universal love. It is the creative energy that gives life, love and perfect health. Everything that this force gives is unconditional. This is why we call it pure energy, pure light. It gives, not because it demands anything back, but purely for the joy of giving.

' "Humanity's wrong thinking will never negate this force. The *human body has emotions that often pull people away from the light. Ignorance, fear and pain cause negativity. This gives a grey, sometimes black appearance. The spirit body lightens when you evolve. It lightens whether you are spirit still in your body or pure spirit. You leave behind those fearful emotions that have the very real effect of weighing you down.*

'"Knowledge plus awareness and truth equals enlightenment.

'"The creative force of unconditional love is devoid of emotion. Unlike the love that some people mistakenly believe is true love, it demands nothing back. On the other hand, our emotions demand and expect a return. We put conditions on what we give and what we do for others. When that which is expected is not forthcoming, we become upset and hit out at others or in at ourselves, creating a conflict that pulls us further away from the inherent truth that is within us all.

'"It's understandable that people believe in two forces — one evil, one good. It is difficult for them to comprehend that the journey through the blackest night must be undertaken to live eternally in the sunniest days. As I guide Miriam, others guide her grand-daughter. She will not be caught up in the dark energy that comes from other people's wrong thinking.

'"People remember their journey into the light for many reasons. It is not only for their own education; it is so that they will re-tell their stories, educating, re-awakening this truth that lies dormant within the minds of all humanity."

'He guided Miriam to a dimension in the tunnel where she was waiting when her grand-daughter arrived. They sat in a beautiful garden full of the scent of roses and they talked to the beautiful being who convinced her to return to earth. He taught Miriam ways in which she could monitor her grand-daughter's progress and impress her with uplifting thoughts, so that now her grand-daughter can feel and sometimes hear Miriam when she's around. He also instructed Miriam on better ways to communicate with people on earth, and she passed those teachings on to us.'

'But, Grandma Edna, I don't want to wait a long time before I can let them know that I am all right.'

'You don't have to wait, dear. There are plenty of opportunities

for us to give messages to people on earth. There are people they call mediums who help the people in the spirit world, and some of these mediums have special gatherings where they talk to a lot of spirit people and pass these messages on to their loved ones on earth. We will go to one of these meetings, but I must warn you that it is not easy to get a message through. You could go many, many times before this happens, and yet sometimes it can happen on your first visit.'

'But how do we know where to go and when?'

'Only those spirits who have the desire to communicate with earth can go. When it's time, you feel everyone's thoughts. It's a process where all who want the same things are drawn together. It's as if we are of one mind. We meet at a place that looks like an enormous amphitheatre and, even if you don't connect to your own people on earth to give them a message, you can learn so much every time you go there.'

'But, Edna, when I was alive I never went to a place like that, and I know Mum hasn't. How can I contact her when she doesn't know of the existence of such a place?' Paula asked.

Edna replied, 'Because of desire and need, the same principles of collective thoughts also apply to people on earth. From the time you entered the spirit world, your thoughts have been constantly of your mother and she has never had you out of her mind. When you are in a physical body, you are not aware that the power of your thoughts has the ability to draw happenings to you. The reality is that our thoughts are a powerful force.

'There are many ways that your mother, through what she calls coincidence, can find herself open to communication from you. She may turn her radio on at exactly the time she hears a mother receiving proof from her dead daughter that she has survived death. A friend may give her a book to read that opens her mind up to the spirit world. She could open a magazine at an article where someone is telling about their near-death experiences. There are numerous ways for a person to become more tuned in. Saying that God works in mysterious ways becomes so much more meaningful when you start learning about this process called "life after death".'

'Edna, all of a sudden I'm feeling excited, and a great sense of

joy has washed over me. I'm going to talk to Mum, I know I am.'

'Yes, dear, it's time to go.'

Edna had no sooner said those words and we were there. No process of transport or having to ask for directions. One second the awareness, the next second the reality. I'm in a place that resembles a football stadium. There's a loud buzzing through the air, the environment is charged with anticipation, excitement and happiness. There are all different types of people. Some are very loud and extremely noisy. These people all seem to be at the front.

My gaze wanders up at the rows of seats, and I become aware of other people. The colours are incredible; they look like a rainbow of every colour I have ever seen, except that they are more vibrant and have more depth. It is so beautiful, it is as if everyone has these colours coming from their bodies. I cannot see the people seated at the top, I can only see their outlines. It's as if a golden haze of light is coming from them and transfuses all the other colours right down to where the noisy people are. It's like a golden halo and is making those people who are emitting it almost transparent.

'Grandmother, who are those people?' I ask.

'Us', she replies. 'They are at a stage of awareness and in a dimension where we one day will find ourselves. We are all God's children learning and growing. You can feel the love coming from them. It gives you a serenity that fills your whole being and it helps quiet those who make so much noise.'

'Grandmother, who is that lady over there waving to you?'

'She was a neighbour and friend of your mother's. She died before you were born. If you are able to communicate with your mother, people whom your mother knew can tune into your vibration and use that connection to say hello. They might only be able to get their name through, but that's enough to make Mum realise that what's happening is not just her wishful thinking or her desire to hear from her daughter or the medium's use of some mind-reading process — because the last person on Mum's mind, the last person she would expect to hear from is that neighbour.'

'Will you talk to Mum, Grandmother?'

'I will certainly try. It's not an easy process. I have tried in

*many different ways before, but there are people who will help us
and tell us what to do. Now, Paula, if you become too excited or
upset, it sends waves like bolts of lightning through the air and
the medium who gives the messages cannot understand you.'*

*All of a sudden, I feel a rocking sensation and Edna's voice is
lost to me. I am aware of a stillness around me that was not there
before and, at the same time, I'm starting to feel as if I am on a
boat, no longer standing next to my grandmother.*

*I am moving without any thought or command on my part. I
can see shapes of people as I am being drawn to them. The beautiful lights and colours of their auras let me know everything is
alright. I feel as if I am being tossed in a sea devoid of water, yet
it's the exact same feeling one experiences when sailing on the
ocean. Then, the moment before stepping on to solid ground, the
tide ebbs, the waves calm, the sea becomes tranquil. I am no longer
subject to those uncertain tides that make up this ocean of human
emotions. In the space of a moment in time they can be the prelude
to a hurricane so devastating in its anger that it eliminates everything in its path; or the prelude to an immense stillness that brings
with it a calmness of the soul — a tranquillity, a serenity that one
can only experience when peace enters the soul.*

*I am feeling an at-oneness as I draw closer to these beautiful
beings. All of my senses sharpen and heighten; everything takes
on a clarity unlike anything I have experienced previously. I am
now part of these swelling, vibrant, indescribable colours. I can see
my mother. It's as if I am looking through a constantly moving
maze of energy, interspersed with faces, scenes of places, voices and
more colours.*

*My mother is reaching out to me. I feel her longing, her every
emotion, her love, the pain caused by my loss. The sadness over-
whelms me and in that instant the waves start, and feelings of
despair cause the atmosphere to become dark and clouded.*

*I start to panic; I don't want to lose her. I am immersed in a
magnificent gold/pink light. It is as if a lifeline has been put around
me and at the same time it encompasses Mum. I am becoming
aware of a steadiness and strong, reassuring feelings. A vibrating
light pulls me closer as if I am in a channel of light, a still and*

calm part of the ocean drawing me closer to where I can feel and hear my mother.

I am now aware that there are spirit people guiding me to this place. They become clearer to me; the gold/pink colour now takes on the appearance of faces and bodies. They are telling me to relax and trust them. A vortex of colour enmeshes me as if I'm in a web, alive and vibrating. I feel as if I am a part of someone else. It's as if the space that is inhabited by my being is now being shared with another person.

I am aware that it is a female, and now I know that it is a woman who is alive and living on the earth plane. The feeling of sharing her body becomes clearer. It is in fact a blending of minds and at the same time a retaining of our own individuality. Her thoughts are talking to me and to my mother. I can't help it; I become so excited when I realise that she can hear me, I cause the waves to start again. This causes my responses to be carried away and the lady cannot hear me. I quickly quiet my thoughts and all is calm again, allowing the lady to tell Mum what I am saying.

Then Grandmother Edna is standing next to me. She gives her name and the lady asks Mum if she knows Edna.

'Yes,' Mum replies. 'That's my grandmother,' she adds excitedly. 'She's my mother's mum.'

Then Norma sings out her name and the lady, whom I later found out is called a medium, repeats the name to Mum.

'No, I don't know her,' comes Mum's reply.

The medium asks Mum not to discount the name and to think about it later and check with other family members. Too soon it is all over, but I feel wonderful and I know Mum is happier, knowing I am alright and not alone.

Now I want to help other people who have just arrived in my world, but before I can do that I have to learn a lot more about myself, my real self.

⤞⤝

Paula now works a lot with kids her own age who pass over as a result of tragedy. She is also one of my spirit helpers.

11

$\mathscr{D}$EATH AND OUR CHILDREN

JUST AS WE HAVE A DUTY TO TEACH our children about life, so too we must give them good and sensible information about death. In the recent past children were very sheltered from death and, when there had to be an explanation, they were told their loved one had gone to heaven. Very rarely did they attend the funeral. These days, however, the media ensures they have constant exposure to death in its many forms, from road accidents through to terminally ill children, so much so that it is almost impossible to shield them from this reality. They ask too many questions. While still innocent, interestingly, they have an almost scientific appreciation of life and a quest for answers to their questions. This is all part of their efforts to assimilate their spiritual knowledge from the spirit world and the knowledge of the world they're now in.

Children are intelligent and often understand more than we do about simple, spiritual truths. So when it comes to discussing death with them, simply tell them that life is a gift, that physical life must come to an end at some stage, and that it's a natural process. Sometimes people become ill and this interferes with the natural process of their life span, so they have to leave this world because their body has worn out. Explain that Nanna (or whoever) has gone into a new world. Tell them that the great thing is that they can still feel her around, that all they have to do is to want her to be there. At all times, Nanna can see them and she knows what is happening in their life, but because her body is different now, it's not as easy for her to give them a cuddle or to tuck them in at night.

When a child dies, the pain is often much more acute than at the death of a grandparent. When a child dies, how do we deal with this pain within the family? I would suggest that the parents talk about the life of the deceased child to the other children. Don't try to deny the life or death of the child, but don't canonise the deceased child either. Keep the normality of what that child was: the wonderful, funny things they used to get up to, as well as the naughty moments. As you talk about the child, let the other children join in. You will find they start to lead the way, and you will gain further insight as to how they are feeling and thinking.

Always remember to point out the effect the passing of that child has on friends, relatives and neighbours. A child draws from its own experiences of what has happened and fully realises that even in death, there are lessons to be learned. They are learning about a world beyond their own. If you don't have answers, don't be afraid to say you don't know. At the same time, let them know that love never dies and so, no matter where the deceased child is, they continue to be brothers and sisters for all time.

Preserving a deceased child's room or clothes is not necessary because, while circumstances are ever-changing, a life never really dies. Possessions don't mean a thing. Children who have gone are not missing one thing from this earth plane – they can reproduce their favourite toys, their bedroom or whatever they want in spirit. Whenever they want it, they can get the buzz from the people they love who they've left behind – except that now they can feel love in a way they were never able to feel it when they were alive. They access the love we have for them because that love resides always in our hearts. It's there for them to draw on whenever they wish it.

The death of teenagers or older children often has added pain brought about by the frustrations of parenting. Bereaved parents are all too aware of the angry words and scenes that have gone on before. But they should take comfort in the knowledge that their children are now feeling an outpouring of love such as they never experienced when they were alive. They are able to feel, and know, the love that resides in a parent's heart. Parents' love for their children, whether they are alive or in spirit, is all-enduring. It doesn't lessen with the passing of time, and it doesn't depend on the keeping of their things. The truth is, when we hang on to our pain by hanging on to material things, we distress those who have passed over.

As the years pass there will always be those moments – in the look of another family member, or on seeing a game or place they loved – when the beautiful memories of that person come flooding back to us. The wonderful thing is that no one can diminish or take away what resides in our hearts.

Losing a child is hard, very hard. Naturally, there are so many questions parents want to ask. When a child dies suddenly, especially violently, they feel no pain. At the moment of impact, the spirit is propelled from the body with such force and speed that it happens quicker than a blink of the eye. Quite often, the victims are so disoriented they don't remember what has just happened to them. This experience is similar to what we feel when we've had a big shock in our physical body.

The child also goes down the tunnel, but very quickly. It is not the same experience as for adults. And as the spirit world is for them a recent memory, returning to spirit is that much easier. As the child assimilates to their surroundings, they become aware of the vibrant colours and beautiful music that resonates through and around them. At the same time, loving and familiar arms enfold them. In cases where the child hasn't lost a parent, grandparent or someone close in their lifetime, angels or other beings will make the child feel safe and secure. Whatever is needed to console manifests before the child in their new world. This could even be a favourite cartoon character or Santa.

The assimilation process for children in the spirit world is everything that human children would think of as 'all their Christmases coming at once'. All the beautiful and fantastic things they might wish for surround them. And the process of assimilation is much quicker for them than for adults. They left home in spirit to come to earth and, little by little, earth became familiar. They grew to love and depend on their parents. It doesn't take long after they return, however, before they again understand the divine law of things. These little souls have returned to a world that is basically their true home. Not one child is lost, wandering or lonely. Of course, there are times when they miss Mum, Dad and family, but there is no doubt, no question in their minds that they will all be together again.

Their journey back to spirit completed, they become a guiding influence for close relatives on the earth plane. Should a parent or relative ever see them, they will show up as a child. However, their spirit might be quite old and wise. Again, as with those miscarried, generally they didn't need the full life on earth to complete that particular cycle of growth.

❧

When people in spirit discover someone who is more psychically developed, someone who can actually hear them, they do their best to use that person to get through to their loved ones. Many try very, very hard to get through to those they love, to let them know they are all right. Imagine when the moment of opportunity finally arrives. Imagine their frustrations, their fear, their excitement at having found a channel to get through.

On the earth plane, people have a similar eagerness to make contact and communicate. It is only natural, for example, that parents who have lost children, particularly in distressing circumstances, want to know that their children are safe and well.

Anthony came to see me because he wanted a message from his eight-year-old son, Brendon, who had died only two weeks before. Brendon appeared, showing me a brown-coloured teddy bear. The bear, it transpired, was his favourite teddy bear, which he slept with each night and which was placed with him in his coffin. Brendon had a fun-loving, mischievous personality and was a giggler. He appeared next to an older man, Anthony's father and Brendon's grandad, who had passed over two years before. Brendon had been and clearly continued to be the light of his grandfather's life.

Brendon was able to tell his father that it wasn't his fault he had died. He showed me a small park on a corner, with him standing on the footpath next to the road. Cars were parked alongside the curb. Brendon went to step out, looking first to the left, then to the right, then to the left again.

Brendon had been hit by a car as he was crossing the road after playing in the neighbourhood park. He'd been trained in road safety from the moment he was old enough to understand and was so careful about crossing the road that he often shepherded younger children back across the road from the park as well. And even though Brendon's house was directly opposite the park, he was so cautious that he often took longer to get home than other kids. It was even a joke among family and friends as to how Brendon wouldn't take a step without first looking left, right and left again.

When the car hit Brendon, he died instantly. The driver said Brendon had run out in front of his car and hadn't stopped to look. No one believed the driver, but there were no witnesses, so there was little that could be done. Now, however, his father knew that Brendon had been taking care as usual, and that the accident was not his fault.

As I continued to describe what I saw to Anthony, he became distraught. Then, as if to lighten the moment for his dad, Brendon started laughing again and showed me a photo of himself in a picture frame. He asked me to tell his dad that he's the one who keeps moving the frame.

'I keep touching Mum's hair too,' he confessed.

Anthony's work involved a lot of travel; staying in hotel rooms was a normal part of his life. He always packed photos of his wife and Brendon to take with him. One photo he took was of his wife and Brendon and the other was of Brendon on his own. He always placed the photos beside his bed in the hotel room.

The day his son died, Anthony found Brendon's photo on the

floor beside the bed. He put the same photo on his bedside table at home, and each night before he and his wife went to sleep, he'd look at the upright photo and ask Brendon to give him a sign if he was alright.

When they awoke each morning, the photo would be face down on the bedside table. Every day, Anthony's wife would tell him she could feel something blowing her hair as if it were being played with. She couldn't feel a hand on her hair and described the sensation as more like a breeze – except there was no breeze around. This sensation was always in the same spot on her head. Often when he was alive and in a playful mood, Brendon would ruffle his mother's hair in that very same place.

༼ঞ༽

Sometimes, dreadful things happen that were not meant to take place. But there will always be compensation for these terrible events, even if we are not aware of what this might be. This is the true meaning of God's perfect plan – that there is no cause without effect. And always, the effects of lives reach far beyond the person concerned. When souls pass on as children or teen-agers, they may touch far more lives than if they were to pass over when they were old.

This brings us to the painful issue of suicide, and the questions that haunt the friends and relatives left behind. On a purely prac-tical level, those who commit suicide do so because they are unable to face the highs and lows of life. The majority of souls who choose this way out have lost the balance within their nature that enables them to cope with life's more difficult moments.

It is important to realise that there is no form of punishment in the universe other than self-punishment. When souls realise they have opted out of the life they in fact chose, they experi-ence a definite sense of remorse at the lost opportunities for growth and learning. Because of this remorse, some of these souls become lost for a time on their way to the spirit world.

They feel the grief of parents and are also shocked at the anguish of all those whom they never imagined cared. This tends to hold them in limbo for a while but, even when in the limbo state, they are not alone. It is important to realise that this limbo is self-imposed. Souls only remain in this place as long as they are wrapped up in their own anguish. As their anguish recedes, they begin to reach out beyond themselves. Then the spirit helpers, who are ready and waiting, can assist them on their way to spirit with great love.

Their spirit guides and the anxious prayers of the loved ones left behind create a protection around these souls, attracting helpers in the spirit world who will take them out of their anguish and on to a far happier place. Then, when they are ready, they can review their life and their final decisions without the emotions they experienced while living. Through this process, they have the opportunity to learn and to grow.

సౖౖ

People also ask me how long we stay in the spirit world before we come back to live on earth each time. There is no easy answer to this. Time is meaningless for us, once we are in spirit. We come back when we are ready to continue our learning and growth on the earth plane; and the time factor is partly governed by our personality. If we are the type who rushes into things, we are likely to return more quickly; those who deliberate might remain in spirit much longer.

In my experience, though, most of us stay in the spirit world for several decades at least. When I am doing readings, it is common for me to meet parents and grandparents who have passed on.

Of course, there are exceptions. A baby or young child might choose to come back quickly, in order to continue their journey on earth.

Whatever timing we choose each time, we can be sure it will be right. With each life on the earth plane, we learn valuable lessons and make progress on our spiritual journey.

Again, the opportunities for healing pain and hurt and disappointment are always there for us. There is often a great deal of pain surrounding the death of those we know. Often we are dealing not only with the loss of that person, but with many unresolved issues around their death. Perhaps we didn't get the opportunity to say goodbye, or perhaps we never got the chance to resolve old quarrels.

What we need to realise is that we are able to have an ongoing relationship with those who are passed over; we can still say our goodbyes or say sorry. Just as our relationship with those we love continues on, so too does the opportunity for healing.

How does this work? Well, it's very much like healing the hiccups we have in our day-to-day lives with those around us. We weigh up what it is that we need to say to the person concerned, then find the opportunity to apologise.

Admittedly, it takes a lot of faith when we first start talking to someone we cannot see or hear. Remember, for them to hear us, we do not need to have a verbal conversation with the people who have passed over. All we need to do is concentrate our thoughts on that deceased person and we are then communicating, because they can hear our thoughts. Just a few simple words are enough.

We may have to go over the same process for a long time to feel we've got through, but it's worthwhile. If you keep an open mind and start this simple experiment, sooner or later you will find your own proof that you have achieved that goodbye or sense of forgiveness you needed.

12

ONGOING OPPORTUNITIES TO GROW

I'M OFTEN ASKED IF WE HAVE A LIFE REVIEW once we're in spirit, and the answer is yes. Nothing we do or say is ever lost. Each of us registers every thought and action, as well as the effects that other people's thoughts and actions have on us. This is part of the concept that God sees and knows all, that not a sparrow falls that he doesn't know about.

When we do access this life review information on the other side, it is only when we are ready for it. There are guides with us when this takes place, because it is such a profound experience. No one would ever have a complete life review at one time. It all depends on the person's nature. Types who hold on to things will take a lot longer to go through one life review, let alone have the opportunity to work on other life reviews.

We all have an in-built never-ending mechanism of recording and replay, like a video machine. This mechanism works throughout our lives on earth, as well as beyond it. We also have the ability, during our time on earth, to draw on this detailed material, but generally we don't. However, we might suddenly feel guilty about a forgotten incident that took place some years before and, all at once, we remember in vivid detail everything that happened. As with all life experiences, there is an opportunity to learn. Some people choose to look at this material, and others block it out. We are also able to access previous lives with such detail.

While past life therapy can be helpful, it should be approached as a tool on the voyage of discovery, and not as the answer. We might recall a lifetime in great detail, and yet, because of our access to the lives of others in the spirit world, we cannot assume that the lifetime we're accessing was in fact ours. The therapist we are with during this process needs to ask the right questions to ascertain whether it is in fact our own life or one we were participating in as a learning experience.

Knowledge is limitless. In spirit we have access to many lives – both those who are living and those who have lived on earth. These are not necessarily just the lives of friends and relatives, but a vast range of people who, through their life experiences, can teach us as we watch the way they behave and the decisions they make. Often we feel alone in our life experience, but one of the many valuable lessons we learn by observing the lives of others is that there is not a thought, feeling or action that countless others have not experienced at other times and in other places.

What does that life review feel like once we are in spirit? We're bystanders in the scenes of our own life or that of another. We are able to see and feel our own feelings during the review process, but we also experience the viewpoints and feelings everyone else had in that same situation.

And so, when we replay the particular situation we're being given access to, we're aware of the effect of our thoughts and words on others. We then become aware that there is nothing in the universe that is not connected to the whole. We'll feel the fear and pain even of the tree that is chopped down. If we have been a loving person during life, we will get all the love back that we gave out and more.

I often see those in spirit shocked at the effect some small act of kindness had on another life. Even one act of kindness that most people don't think twice about can have a profound result.

And so, just making a cup of tea for the lady next door – giving of ourselves in such simple ways – has great blessing attached to it for everyone concerned. This is the true meaning of the joy of giving, of being there for another person.

The other side of this is being able to forgive ourselves our shortcomings and then going forward in life. During the process of our life review, our guides are with us so we can fairly weigh up what we are being shown, because generally we judge ourselves too critically. When we look back on parts of our life, we forget our circumstances and emotions at the time. Being burdened with guilt is useless because it does nothing constructive. Learning from our shortcomings can be truly blessed, because then we move on.

One of the great stories of a life review is the much-loved *A Christmas Carol*, by Charles Dickens. Its message is that whether we are in spirit or alive makes no difference, for there is always the chance to make amends, and time is allowed for each of us to do this. If we look at the opening scene in *A Christmas Carol*, poor Scrooge is in denial about the first appearance of Marley, his deceased partner. His heart is hardened, and he is in no mood to change his ways. It takes him three nights before he is ready to make amends for past wrongs. Then he is willing, eager even, to change the way he has been behaving and, in doing so, is able to have a profound effect on the lives of those around him.

Ebenezer Scrooge wouldn't have changed without having the opportunity to recognise what he'd done, but at the same time we see the sad moments in his former young life and we feel for this person. The process leading to the change was a gentle one and taken in stages, allowing Scrooge time to reflect. As always, the choice was his to make. In the final scene we see that Scrooge is a changed man, now able to feel joy at saving the life of little Tim by giving the money for an operation. Through his change of heart, there is joy for everyone.

Getting on a bus and smiling at someone, or getting up to give a person our seat, could even save a life. This might sound far-fetched, but the person whose life we have just touched by our kind action could have been contemplating suicide, and our one kind gesture might make them feel worthwhile enough to give life another go. In that one brief moment of kindness, we've lightened the energy around someone who desperately needed that.

There will be some people we feel unable to love, and this is quite human. What we must learn to do in these situations is to tolerate another's defects and to rejoice in their accomplishments.

We also need to be aware of how piercing is the spiteful word, the angry aside. A great deal has been said about karma. It's a very straightforward concept: ultimately, in all our actions, whatever we do to others we are in fact doing to ourselves. If we create kindness, sooner or later we'll experience the measure of that kindness. The reverse is also true. The most important thing is that we inhabit a loving universe and, no matter how misguided we've been, there is always the opportunity for change.

≈

I am often asked if there is a hell. The answer is yes and no. Yes, there are realms in the spirit world for misguided souls, but there is no hellfire and brimstone. Souls remain in these regions only as long as they are unaware that there is something beyond where they are.

Imagine a world where the sun and sky are permanently overcast with heavy dark clouds that close out all the light. A never-ending flow of people is passing through this place. Some are not even aware they are travelling in this area because they are moving so quickly towards a light that is unseen by the inhabitants of this world. This light creates a vortex of lighter, colourful energy. It is not unlike catching an express elevator from the first floor to the third floor. The occupants of the lift are unaware or unconcerned about the second floor or the people who occupy that second floor, let alone what it looks like, because they are focused on getting to the third floor.

Some people do stop and get off at the second floor, but quickly discover that they don't belong there. They don't want to stay, so they resume their journey. Others think this is where they belong and, because their thoughts and attitudes are negative, they feel at home. Still others are so riddled with guilt because of acts they have committed when they were alive that they, too, feel at home in this place.

This is not a place of punishment or, at least not in the way we've been led to believe in teachings of hell. It's all to do with vibrations again. Those who feel comfortable in this place are those whose vibrations match its heavy atmosphere. Some stay longer than others, not realising at first that it is their own thinking processes that create this darkness and keep them there.

The very clouds that stop the light and prevent souls from moving on are partly held in place by their own negative thoughts. Other souls remain because they are still holding tightly to unforgiving religious or other belief systems. They believe this place to be their punishment.

Because this dimension is a part of our earth plane and all thoughts have an energy of their own, these negative spirits are able to project their energies onto the thoughts of those living on earth, and so continue to add to the darkness of this world. This does not mean that we have need for concern, because their negative energy is only taken up by like-minded souls in this world. Like attracts like.

～～～

How do we begin to understand these different dimensions in which we live? There are so many of them, and our experiences of them vary as our journey progresses. But there are really three main areas: the earth plane, the transitional dimensions, and the astral.

The earth plane is the only dimension in which we take on a solid physical form. When we die, we pass through the transitional dimensions, which include both dark and light. The dark dimensions are often called the lower astral, sometimes described as Hell. They are very unpleasant places, and those of us who are positive in outlook and unburdened by negative emotions pass through so swiftly that we have little or no recollection of this darkness. The light transitional, sometimes referred to as Summerland, allows us to take stock and adjust to the realisation that we have returned to the spirit world.

From here, we travel to the astral – those dimensions that are the spirit world, where time and space do not exist, and where we continue to live and grow in the light.

Those of us on the earth plane are able to access the other dimensions, and this becomes easier as we develop our psychic abilities. A word of warning: the dark dimension is not to be played around with. I understand why people who play with Ouija boards as a party game can end up losing their minds. The dark dimension is devoid of colour and is made up of all the things that constitute our worst nightmares.

Firstly, dark spirits will give information about people or events in a person's life, making the novice believe they are in contact with some all-knowing entity. We might be told it's a relative whom we yearn to hear from or some well-known personage or religious figure, perhaps a saint or even Jesus Christ. Anything is used that will impress the listener and enable the mischievous spirits to gain control of their thinking. People become hooked on getting messages.

The next thing we know, we cannot get a good night's sleep because the mischievous spirits keep waking us up. They start interfering with our thinking process when we are trying to go about our daily working life. Slowly but surely, all of our defences are being weakened. We are being told that the end of the world is imminent. These are all mind games that work on our fears.

Fortunately, I came from a solid base and have life-long teachers in spirit who are gentle, loving and kind. Spirit beings have never frightened me, because I have been taught to understand what is happening. There is no need for fear if you understand what is going on.

I have come to understand the power of our thoughts and the very important difference between imagination and reality. I know that spirit beings cannot cause physical harm. They can, however, create their own realities, good and bad, which they project as feelings into a living person's reality. These might be feelings of joy and peace or of fear and anxiety. Having been confronted with all the lower astral tricks, I now realise that my sense of humour helped a great deal, and I learned the importance of being fearless and asking the right questions.

The same principle applies here as when we first meet someone. It depends on what we expect from a friend or colleague. We are all products of our own experiences. If we like being told what to do, then we will accept a personality that does our thinking for us. If that's unacceptable, then we reject it. If our first thoughts are how we can use another person, then those are the individuals we attract. If we want power over people, then we will attract entities that seek power over others.

But there are always willing workers in the spirit world. They are happy to help those who are lost in that region called the lower astral, the lost souls who are fearful and distrust everyone. The longer they are away from the light, still struggling with the energies that need to be left behind when they leave this world, the harder it is for them to find their way. This is because they cling to the familiar, to being on the earth plane.

To move on, they need to separate themselves completely from this attachment; it causes a weakening of their energy, similar to the feelings of tiredness and weakness we feel when we are ill. The enlightened spirits are always there to help, but sometimes they find it difficult to do so.

The process is similar to a person drowning in the ocean. When the drowning person starts fighting the rescuers, it makes the rescue very difficult. However, the weaker they become, the easier it is to rescue them. The medium's role is that of the rescuer. When a medium is not available, the rescue can take much longer. Either way, help is always available to all souls.

⤝⤞

Where do ideas come from? The spark of an idea may be planted by spirit intervention, when someone from the spirit world decides the time is right. Or an event on earth can be the catalyst for releasing a memory from a past life, and bringing it closer to the surface again. When the subconscious mind ignites the spark that is the beginning of an idea, it spreads like a small, slow fire. It may emerge either as a dream or appear to spring randomly into our conscious mind. This in turn causes a flicker of inspiration that fuels the imagination. This new idea reaches the conscious mind, where the ego holds on to it in the form of a dream, goal or fantasy. Or perhaps we decide to expend the energy there and then to make it happen.

Normal, balanced people are able to think through thoughts or ideas, keeping only those that appeal to their nature, and throwing out those that don't fit with their balanced mind or belief system. The problems start when unbalanced people accept these thoughts as their own. When these thoughts are brought into real life, because it's the same process for everyone, humankind is either greatly uplifted or experiences unbelievable suffering. Two men who are examples of this process of positive and negative energy thoughts are Abraham Lincoln and Adolf Hitler respectively.

From the time people first set foot on this earth, they inadvertently accessed the dimension called hell (the lower astral). Never before has it been as evident as it is today. The availability of mind-altering drugs, alcohol, wrong information given in psychic development classes and wrong meditation techniques all allow the negative energy to gain hold in our world. There are also people without the necessary spiritual training setting themselves up to do professional readings. Without this training, they do not know how to protect themselves and their clients from the negative forces.

Millions of people are going to the movies to watch violence and horror in the name of entertainment, and turning the television on to subject themselves to that constant stream of negativity. The subliminal messages given by certain kinds of music and the constant unhealthy stimulation of some computer games all affect the subconscious mind and cause imbalance.

This imbalance then opens people up to the world called the lower astral or hell. One of the most common examples of this is the number of people who say they hear voices telling them it is God or Jesus talking, ordering them to kill. The terrible thing is that some listen to those voices.

The best way to take the fear and mystery out of the spirit world and its inhabitants is to remind yourself that they are people. Anyone who has any understanding of human nature quickly discovers that death has not changed the personalities and attitudes of the inhabitants of the lower astral.

Freeing ourselves from fear not only makes our physical body and mind feel free; it lightens and uplifts the energy we project, and people feel good around us. When we rid ourselves of fear, we are actually projecting a healing energy, which is healing and helping others at the same time that it is healing us.

People who don't understand the use of the word energy should think of attitude. A person's state of mind, whether happy, sad, morbid or cranky, creates an atmosphere around that individual. When we spend time with people, we are affected by their energy, by their attitude. And if we are particularly sensitive, we find ourselves uplifted or depressed according to what the other person is like. In this kind of situation we may find that the other person's reality has become ours; that person's energy has intruded into our world.

Those people who understand that our thoughts create a particular energy know that through prayer and meditation, through simply visualising the white light and visualising a world full of love and peace, we not only combat the darkness, we annihilate it. We must remember always that where there is light, there cannot be darkness.

13

$\mathcal{A}$BOUT PSYCHIC ABILITIES

THE QUESTION I AM CONTINUALLY ASKED IS: 'How do you do it?' The simple answer is that even the people who experience psychic phenomenon have no more understanding about how it works than one who has never experienced it. Just as our personalities are individual and unique, so is the way we receive and filter information. I have never had what is classed as a 'normal' life. There was never an awakening or discovery of my psychic abilities; I have been aware of them all my life.

I don't have any fanatical religious beliefs; nor do I have an unquestioning faith. What I know comes from talking to normal everyday people who have died. All my life, I have asked questions. Since I have an inquiring mind, I have received a great many answers to my many questions. My knowledge has been gained through information given to me. I have had to wait a long time, however, before I could talk openly about this subject.

As we walk the path of enlightenment, it is a normal process for our sensitivity to increase. Our psychic awareness will grow until we come to realise that we are indeed masters of our own destiny.

I became a minister of a spiritualist religion because it taught what I already knew in my heart was the truth. I have always said that demonstrating my psychic abilities is the frosting on the cake. We taste it and we want more.

People take notice when you give them readings. Then, after a while, they start to ask questions. Many realise that they have been having their own psychic experiences throughout their lives. They then become aware of the spiritual aspects of their natures. This leads them to discover spiritual truths, to realise that we are all on the same path of growth, awareness and enlightenment.

My interpretation of a psychic is someone who tunes into psychic energy, someone who can see the future, the past and the present. They might see events in their own lives and the lives of people around them; or they might see world events. If untrained, they will have flashes or inconsistent times of 'intunement'. They are prone to pick up negative aspects, such as plane crashes, earthquakes, car accidents, a death in the family or in the workplace.

Why does this happen? Imagine you are standing in the middle of a city street. It's late at night and there is no lighting. You are holding a flashlight in your hand. You drop the light and it rolls and spins out of control, making its own way down the street ahead of you, distorting everything in its path, so that it is impossible for you to correctly assess your surroundings. You try to reassure yourself that the grotesque shapes that flicker before your eyes are your imagination. As you run after the light, your mind is centred on retrieving the torch quickly so that you can take control. The momentary glimpses of scenes that light up for a split second are your only reality. The interpretation is up to you.

If you are a person with a huge amount of commonsense and are not ruled by fear, you will logically assess your environment. On the other hand if, in your normal world, you are full of self-doubt and fear, you will see death, destruction or ghosts every time that flashlight lights up any area or scene in the street.

People who have not developed any spiritual understanding will tend to interpret everything they tune into as negative. They will continually predict gloom and doom. Fear overcomes them.

It rules them, so that they turn and run in the opposite direction rather than gaining control of the light. For the rest of their lives, they carry the memories of that incident deeply impregnated in their subconscious mind. Every time their psychic faculties are triggered, they see gloom and doom.

This problem can be overcome through education. However, it is almost impossible to help someone like this when they insist on doing psychic readings for other people. Fear is like a plague; it spreads throughout human minds and bodies. If left untreated, it erodes the soul.

Clairvoyance means clear sight and is one aspect of psychic ability. Others include being able to see spirit beings, hear spirit voices and even see auras or parts of auras.

The aura is the magnetic field that emanates from and surrounds all things. Human auras are different in colour and vibration from those of domestic pets. Plants and trees are different again. Their colour vibration and energy is less static and has a shared consciousness or life force that lacks individual souls and separate intelligence. You can look at a mountain or any expanse of water and see the aura of colour around these scenes. This is their life force and if there are animals on the mountain, or fish in the water, the vibrations of these additional life forces send forth their own energy fields with their particular colours.

It is the same principle as human beings having fingerprints. Everything in the universe has a vibration of energy and colour that identifies its species. Add this to the energy colour of the mountain, or whatever, and we have a story in colour telling us what animals, insects and other life forms inhabit that particular area.

The aura of an inanimate object lacks life; the colour around such an object is dull and presents itself as a creamy or very light yellow. With all living things, however, the aura takes on a shimmering, moving effect. You could liken it to an electrical current that has four basic colours – blue, green, red and yellow. One rule applies to all living things: when one colour predominates, if that colour is dull or murky, it is a barometer for health problems.

In human beings, there are many other colours that present themselves through the aura. This is because humankind has intelligence and emotions that create many different moods. Add to this our ability to feel and inflict pain, to be inspired and to inspire, and you can see why the pattern of colours is more complex. All of these processes emit particular energies that have a colour peculiar to those energies. The aura is an energy field constantly vibrating with the electrical charges that each person emits, in a similar fashion to the way a conductor transmits electricity. A human person's aura is a kaleidoscope of colour and is ever-changing.

Clairvoyants are able to see or sense the predominance of a certain colour in a person's body and, if trained correctly, can become skilled in diagnosing existing and future health problems. They can also become excellent healers. Untrained, they have moments of vision, moments of seeing auras. If fear takes over, it can easily lead to paranoia, schizophrenia, behavioural problems, or phobias – the person may be afraid of the dark or forever feel that someone is watching them.

Without careful training, people with clairvoyance are so open to negative aspects of the psychic areas that socialising with normal people is a thing of the past. The belief that everyone is talking behind their back and sending negative energy is common. So is feeling aches and pains in the body. If there is no one to help the student understand what is happening and how to close off, the results can be devastating. Symptoms of every illness known to man start to manifest in the body. If a doctor is consulted and tests ordered, a long, painful and costly journey is undertaken and at the end, all the tests show clear results. However, the pain of a heart condition, brain tumour, kidney problem or whatever is still there and the patient is told the symptoms are in their mind or due to stress.

Quite often when a crime is committed and the perpetrator tells us that God or voices told him to do it, he is telling the truth. This is an example of the clairvoyant faculty of the psychic nature opening up prematurely. The nature of the person is unbalanced in the first place, making it impossible for knowledge to be gained on spiritual principles, so there is no way to distinguish reality from psychic impressions. The person has no training so cannot close off or shut out the bombardment. Inevitably, their mind becomes completely unbalanced.

A medium is the go-between for transmitting teachings and messages from other dimensions. This can take many forms. One is called trance. Spirit beings talk to and materialise through the body of the medium for the purpose of enlightening mankind.

The conducting of these energies is like using an electrical cord. You plug it into any electrical appliance. You have the positive wire, the negative wire and the earth. If the appliance is a washing machine, it will wash and rinse and spin-dry. The clothes will come out clean. The electrical cord cannot understand why or how this process works — it just does. Plug the electrical cord into a television set and it will produce sound and pictures. If one of the wires is faulty, the end result will still be there, but the clothes in the washing machine will not be as clean or dry. The picture on the television set will not be as clear, or the sound may be slightly distorted.

Apply this analogy to mediums. If they are not properly earthed, if they are power hungry, egotistical or religiously fanatical, for example, they will suffer interference and the end result of their messages will be distorted.

Mediums can give information totally alien to them. They can give accurate information about topics they have never studied or read about. No props are needed. No prior knowledge is necessary. The information passes through them from every level. The medium is the combination of all areas: a psychic, a healer, and a clairvoyant. These abilities are the most common, but there are many more.

Our loved ones try many ways to contact us, some more startling than others. One client I saw recently returned home from the funeral of her husband to find a rose sitting in the empty vase she had on the dining room table. She was shocked and dismayed to see this, as the house was locked up and no one could have been in her home while she was out.

But when she thought about it, she came to the conclusion

that it had been her husband trying to get in contact with her. When she subsequently came to see me for a reading, it was her mother who came through. She was quite definite that she had put the rose in the vase. She reminded my bemused client that she was the gardener in the family and that my client's husband wouldn't have known one flower from another. My client couldn't help but laugh at this information – her mother was indeed a superb gardener and her husband scarcely knew one plant from the next.

⌘

Moving or carrying objects from one dimension to another is called apporting. This is another aspect of psychic ability, and is generally carried out by those already in spirit. A whole range of objects and items can be apported. The object is dematerialised and transferred through to the spirit world, then rematerialised back into this dimension, often in another location. When the object returns to this dimension, there is a plopping sound. Jewellery, for example, might be taken from family members or, as improbable as it might sound, it can also be sunken treasure or jewellery that has remained buried in the earth for centuries.

A dear medium friend of mine was always getting apports as a gesture of thanks. They were gifts from spirits who were grateful that she had enabled them to contact loved ones. She had two big old-fashioned chest drawers full of buttons with faces of saints on them, holy pictures with prayers on the back, rings and a whole manner of things.

I remember when I was about seventeen I was in contact with an interesting circle of old spiritualists who were always receiving apports. The circle was run by a herbalist who was able to look at a person's body and diagnose the sickness. He was so exceptional that even local doctors used him for his diagnostic skills.

One morning, I arrived after they'd had a sitting to find the rug in their meeting room had a huge dirty mark on it. A geranium had been apported, dirt and all, and they hadn't been able to get the dirt off the carpet! Some time later, the herbalist took sick one evening with a bad case of the flu. His main guide came to him and said that he needed to rub eucalyptus on his chest. He replied he didn't have any. His guide said they'd get him some eucalyptus oil, and soon after, a bottle of eucalyptus was apported. The interesting thing was that this particular brand of eucalyptus oil wasn't even sold in Australia – and it was labelled 'made in England'!

Around the death of a loved one people often find articles of jewellery go missing, especially rings. The pieces of jewellery that generally vanish are items whose absence would be noticed – jewellery, for example, that is always placed in the same spot after being worn. The owners know they haven't lost the jewellery, and often no one would have had the opportunity to steal it either. When the owners find their way to me, they often ask where the ring is.

I can honestly say, nine times out of ten, I can see that the jewellery has been apported and, inevitably, by a relative who has recently passed away. In those cases, the jewellery will appear again. It might be a week or a year later, but it will be returned.

An American girlfriend of mine had given her father's wedding ring to her husband when they were married. It was a very distinctive wedding band, and her husband wore it all the time. Then, for some reason, he took it off momentarily and it vanished without explanation.

When she asked me about the ring, her father came through from spirit and told me he wanted his daughter to keep his ring. He knew that the marriage was going to break up, so he had taken the ring to ensure it would ultimately remain in his daughter's possession. I didn't give my girlfriend that exact message; at the time, she and her husband thought they were working through their problems. I did tell her, however, that her father had the ring and that it would soon reappear.

Within twelve months, the marriage broke down and they separated. The next time my friend came to me for a reading, her father came through to say that the ring would soon be back in his daughter's possession. Within a week she returned to America and, a couple of weeks later, the ring reappeared.

❧

Those who have passed on use many ways to let us know that life continues in the world of spirit. One of my more humorous moments occurred the day I opened my French doors to a lady who was booked in for a reading. I was more than a little taken aback to find her two golden labrador dogs walking with her into my home. Actually I was a bit put out, as she hadn't asked if I would mind having the dogs present. But I decided not to make a fuss. She made herself comfortable on the sofa and the dogs sat on the floor on either side of her. On we went with the reading until I felt I had to comment on how well behaved her dogs were.

'What dogs?' she asked.

We stared at each other. Then I described the dogs and discovered that these had been the much-loved pets she'd had at different times of her life. One was recently departed and the other was long gone.

Having deceased pets around us is not uncommon. At a recent public event I did an anonymous reading which mentioned a black labrador, a seeing-eye dog. Then I got a message through about another almost identical dog. At that point the audience erupted. The lady for whom I'd been reading turned out to be blind. Her black seeing-eye dog was curled up under her seat out of my line of sight and was the replacement for an earlier, almost identical, black labrador that had recently departed.

On another occasion, a young girl in her twenties, who lived on her own, came to me for a reading. Scarcely had I got started when a white cockatoo landed on her shoulder and started to sneeze. When I mentioned the bird to the girl, she laughed because she'd taught it to sneeze. It was her dearest companion and it had passed over only a week before.

Not everyone is going to get something that definite. But it's important that after losing a loved one we take note of the impressions we receive, whether they be thoughts or a sense of the person we have loved and lost – because often, they are with us. Even if we haven't had a direct experience or message, increasingly today we are able to take comfort from the accounts of others. So often I have had wonderful feedback after doing my radio shows and demonstrations, telling me how comforting it was for people to have the proof again and again that there is life beyond this life. This leads us to the question of ghosts.

A great deal has been written about ghosts, but very little contains any real information. In the case where a particular building is said to be haunted by a ghost or ghosts, the spirit has not made a normal transition from their earthly body. This is because the energy field (aura) that surrounds the spirit body is so greatly impregnated with the heavier, grosser energies of the earthly existence that the person is entrapped in the lower astral, a dark, limbo stage where the person is still aware of the earth dimension. People here are neither wholly in one nor the other. The spirit body is weighed down, so to speak, and the person feels most at home in the environment lived in on earth. The longer and more often the spirits keep appearing in our dimension, the easier it becomes for people to see them.

There are those who do not wish to leave this environment, and they have many different reasons for this. Some seek vengeance; others, justice for a wrong committed against them while they were alive. There are thousands of reasons for not wanting to travel on. Spirits with certain religious beliefs, on finding themselves in the lower astral, believe it is purgatory or limbo and that they are there because they deserve to be punished. It is very difficult to convince these people that they don't have to stay; that they can go on into the light and that it's as easy as a thought. What we believe is our reality.

❦

The man who sat in front of me was nervous and obviously wishing he was not here having a reading. I asked him for his watch and told him to relax, then started to tune in to his life. I saw him in a schoolroom. The students were not children, so I asked him if he was a lecturer. He said he was. Then I became aware of mathematical symbols on the blackboard, so I asked if he taught maths. Again he said, 'Yes', and before my eyes he began visibly to relax.

I started giving him information about his family. His name was Peter, his wife's name was Ann. They had a three-year-old daughter called Amy. Everything was going along in a normal manner, and then I found myself drawn into the family home. The impressions I was getting were at variance with a normal lifestyle and with the appearance of Peter and his family.

I kept talking, trying to fathom what was going on in this home, and then I became aware of a succession of events taking place there. Firstly, the stove was turned on. It was a gas stove and a flame burst high into the air. Then the lights were going on and off, but no human hand was touching the light switch. The fridge door opened and food began falling out, again with no human intervention. Then the radio on the breakfast bar turned itself on and the back door of the kitchen flew open. I had to compose myself so he wouldn't see how upset I was.

'You are having some problems at home,' I said.

He started to cry so I turned off my tape and went into the kitchen to make him a cup of coffee. I welcomed the brief break because I didn't know what I was dealing with. I asked my guides for help as I made the coffee and the answers were given to me.

I went back in to Peter and told him that he was living in a haunted house and that I could find the solution. In fact, I was as much in the dark as he was at that time, and had no idea what the solution could be. I was repeating what my guides had told me. I recommenced the reading and was taken back in time.

I was in his house again, but everything was different. The structure was the same, but the colour and the furniture had changed and there was a wall dividing the kitchen and the dining room. It was a scene from maybe fifty years before. I could see an old lady making a pot of tea and I followed her as she went into the bedroom, where there was an elderly man sitting up in bed. I knew he was her husband. There was a dog, also old and frail, sitting at the end of the bed.

The next moment I was in the same house but at a different time. The old lady was alone and she was grieving for her dead husband, with the dog sitting at her feet. Suddenly, I was shifted ahead in time once more and now the old lady was dead. The house had been sold, but she had not passed on and was still in the house. Then it was revealed to me that the house had been sold five times, the last time being to the present owners, and the old lady was still living there.

I told Peter everything as it was revealed to me. There was much more, of course, but I have just written down the important points. My problem was: what to do to help this family? On the advice of my guides, I arranged to visit the house. We agreed on a time and date, and Peter went home feeling relieved that he had found someone who could help him. I arrived at seven in the evening a week later with my friend, Eileen. We were introduced to Ann, and taken into the kitchen. After asking Peter and Ann to leave, we sat at the table, and I did the only thing I knew to do. I began questioning the old lady. I asked her if she knew the trouble she was causing the occupants of the house. Here is her story:

'It's my home, and people keep coming into it and doing whatever they like, totally disregarding my wishes. They knocked the wall out of the kitchen! I've tried to scare them off by fiddling with the knobs on the stove and turning the lights on and off. They've put that stupid icebox in the wrong place, so I just keep putting their food on the floor. I've even put a glass of water in the middle of the lounge room floor, but nothing moves them. I want my home to myself.'

'But you're dead and this house no longer belongs to you,' I said to her, and continued in that vein. I was surprised to discover that she knew she was dead and couldn't understand why it should make any difference to the ownership of the house. We talked for three and a half hours. What finally persuaded her to go was the appearance of her husband and the little dog. Because she had stayed in this earth's vibration, her husband had been unable to get through to her, but as soon as Eileen and I prayed for her and asked for the white light, there he was to help.

We brought Ann and Peter in and we all said the Lord's Prayer, asking for a blessing on the house and all who lived in it. The glass of water had not come up in the reading I had done for Peter, so I asked them about it. They confirmed that at least once a week, right in the middle of the lounge room, they would find a glass filled to the brim with water.

Peter was a professor of maths and Ann was a teacher. Neither of them had ever had anything to do with the occult or had any belief in spirits or mediums. For two years they had battled with the supernatural disturbances in their home and, in desperation, had come to me.

Peter had never discussed his problems with anyone and feared people would think he was an idiot for coming to a medium. He told himself he was mad and was quite prepared to walk out if he felt the reading was stupid. More than that, he expected me to pump him for information and had to put these doubts to rest when I gave him information without asking a single question.

There are times when it is not necessary to go to people's homes. A reading can often explain what is happening. Judith had come for a private consultation. She was in her mid-seventies. As I started her reading, I commented that she was having problems sleeping. She burst into tears. Trying to regain her composure, she explained her reason for coming to me. For the past three weeks, she had been haunted by a dreadful ghost who kept jumping on her bed at 3 am every day. To make matters worse, she could feel something cold and wet on her face. Not unexpectedly, Judith was terrified and thought at first she was losing her mind. Fortunately, however, she was reassured that something strange was going on because her bedclothes were very dishevelled; when she was awake, she could even watch her bedclothes being messed up.

As Judith continued to talk, a man came from the spirit world and stood beside her. Then, like a bolt of lightning, a big brown dog hopped up on my desk. I jumped, then started to laugh because this big playful spirit dog was doing everything possible to get Judith's attention. Judith meanwhile was completely unaware of the scene taking place in front of her.

I said that I now knew her visitor was no ghost, and started to explain what was going on. I described the man who had joined us; he turned out to be her father who, like Judith, was a dog lover. It transpired that the brown dog was Laddie, her only companion for seventeen years. Every morning when he was alive, Laddie would jump on Judith's bed and lick her face to wake her up. For the last two years of his earthly life, he had become too old to jump on the bed; instead, he would come into the bedroom every morning and bark at her. Laddie had died twelve months earlier, and this was his way of letting his beloved Judith know that he was healthy and young again.

Judith's dad agreed to try to work out some way that Laddie could visit Judith at a reasonable time. She went to bed at 10 pm and got up at 7 am. I talked to her a month later and she informed me that it didn't matter what time Laddie dropped in, now that she knew who it was. She laughed as she told me he continued to visit her, but never at 3 am!

If we are able to understand and accept the different dimensions, life becomes much simpler. We understand much more of what goes on in our earthly lives, and can cope with experiences that otherwise would bring great pain and sadness.

14

ABOUT TOMORROW

THESE DAYS SO MUCH ENERGY IS GIVEN to the future, but sadly, the visions are too often gloomy, to say the least. Will our planet survive or is it headed for extinction? Certainly, we are constantly bombarded with negative, frightening information about the future of our world. We are told that the youth of today are on a path to self-destruction, and yet most of our young people are more spiritually aware than their parents were. They are not afraid to think beyond the confines of society, beyond the belief systems of their parents and grandparents. They are asking questions that the majority of adults didn't even think about when they were young.

Of course our world has problems, and many people feel weighed down and discouraged. Every single thing that happens to any person in this world has an effect on at least one other person and, depending on whether it was a good or bad experience, it also affects those in the vicinity, either positively or negatively. When we consider the extensive media reporting of world events such as natural disasters, vehicle accidents, murders, suicides and so on, we begin to understand how the effects and lessons of these incidents can be felt by millions of people.

It is not unusual for a child to know someone who has died through an overdose of drugs or in a car accident, or to know of someone at their school or in their neighbourhood who has committed suicide. This is unfortunate on one level, and yet there are also positive outcomes. We learn by observing the suffering of those around us, whether the suffering results from their own decisions or the decisions of others. Because of the experiences those people go through, they become our teachers.

It is a very young soul who thinks they have to experience everything personally to be able to learn. The passion and energy of our spiritually aware youth, directed towards a better understanding and application of spiritual principles, are powerful enough to stop wars forever. And when this passion and energy are directed into the area of scientific knowledge, they will stop all forces that have been destructive to mankind.

Consider a recent phenomenon that has swept through our world: the interest, shared by both adults and children, in an extinct life form, the dinosaurs. Science tells us that there are fish, birds and all types of animals inhabiting our modern world that are descended from the dinosaur period. Advances are still being made in palaeontology and archaeology, as new instruments enable scientists to accurately date the period in which the fossils walked the earth as living, breathing creatures. Scientists from different countries are now working together and sharing their knowledge. A child can tell you the names of the numerous dinosaurs, and describe their habitats, their food, the areas of the world they inhabited and much more.

Hundreds of millions of years have passed on this planet and only now is humankind learning how to unravel some of the mysteries of our past. As we find answers, we want to learn more. Because we have intelligence and curiosity, we will invent new machines, new ways to solve the mysteries of extinct civilisations and lost continents. And one of the discoveries we will make is that nothing ceases.

Within every thing that grows – the trees, plants, oceans and every living creature – there is a memory indelibly printed, a blueprint of its origin, telling us how it looked at its time of conception by the Creator. For hundreds of millions of years this truth has lain buried within man's subconscious mind. The planet we live on has its own memory within its rocks, its plants – the story of its creation. Imagine the excitement of discovering that we all have spiritual DNA, that every one of us has the story of our creation, the lives we have lived previously, how we looked, how we lived and where we lived. With these discoveries of the mysteries of creation and evolution, we will come to the understanding that nothing is extinct.

How often do you hear stories of seemingly accidental discoveries preceding major scientific breakthroughs? The scientist who stumbled across a missing link, a fossil or an ancient dwelling by accident? The discovery of the biggest fossil site known to man, which sparked our current preoccupation with the dinosaur, took place in the Gobi Desert. One of the scientists literally tripped and landed in the middle of dinosaur bones. While excavating this site, they found dinosaur eggs, something that had never been seen by modern humankind. Later discoveries revealed previously unknown new species. Throughout scientific history, such stories are not unusual. Nothing is coincidence.

Consider for a moment that this interest, like many others, is, in fact, contrived by teachers in the spirit world. They work ceaselessly to impress on our subconscious minds interests that will advance human progress and understanding, through the use of our imaginations. The implanting of such messages starts people thinking about the positive aspects of why and how, and leads to the discovery of many truths.

An inherent component of human nature is its will, its need and its drive to learn, progress and never stagnate. This guarantees that it will survive, prosper and evolve. People who express their creative energies to the world through music, art, the written word and movies are using a psychic spiritual faculty that is being orchestrated by the universal principle of spiritual truths. Many of these people are unaware that they are spiritual educators and are being used for the uplifting of humankind. Some don't want to think that their ideas are anything other than their own imaginations, yet often the essence of truth is in their work.

Whatever we come across, we must always exercise our

discernment. When questioning anything to do with spiritual matters, for example, we first need to open our minds. We must allow ourselves to go beyond the confines and restrictions of this mortal world, allow the child within to surface, and open our minds to the belief that all things are possible. The analytical mind must not be allowed to negate the inspirational mind; the inspirational mind must be allowed to try, test and re-test the information it receives. Only then is it appropriate to apply the logical, analytical side of the brain.

There have been many movies depicting what happens to people when they die. The writers' and directors' ideas influence the outcome of the story and the messages throughout the movie, affecting people in vastly different ways. Where spiritual truths exist on the screen or through the written word, certain keys are present to trigger our awareness. Because we are individuals and at different soul ages, our perceptions of this material are different.

∽∾

The changes in this world over the past fifty years have been extraordinary. Some are wonderful, others terrifying; all provide lessons for us.

In the West at least, people are free to talk openly about anything they choose. Many groups lobby for and safeguard rights; the liberation of women and the gay community are just two examples. There is only limited fear of being persecuted for one's beliefs.

Indigenous people are finally being recognised. At last they have regained rights to some of their land – a shift indicating that society is beginning to acknowledge their spiritual beliefs. For two hundred years, the Aboriginal people of Australia were denied the right to talk about and openly practise their religion. The deeply embedded spiritual structure which is the foundation of their culture was ridiculed and branded as paganism. Native Americans, who inhabited the rolling plains of the American West for thousands of years before being colonised, now have the freedom to speak out and present their spiritual concepts. They, like their Australian cousins, experience the satisfaction of having the world listen to them on environmental issues.

Through science and education, humankind now knows that the trees must be preserved, that the land must be respected and the waterways kept pure – wisdom that is integral to the fabric of these ancient peoples' cultures and religious beliefs. Western society is slowly catching up and becoming aware that spiritual principles are not hocus pocus to be ridiculed and condemned. Science is beginning to realise that the myths associated with the healing properties of plants are not the product of uneducated minds, that there truly are curative powers in a great many 'natural remedies'. Ancient cultures had access to these laws of nature and realised that they are spiritual laws. People in ancient cultures treated their bodies in a holistic way. There was no separation of the physical self from the spiritual self.

Whatever is to happen, nature is in charge and will always find ways to renew itself. These massive changes to our lives will bring about radically changed ways of living. Where people fail to learn through their individual experiences, they will be forced to learn in other ways. For example, there might be those who have paid no attention to the hungry and have allowed food to be wasted and destroyed. The time will come, with changes in weather, when food will be short and they, too, will experience what it is like not to have enough to eat. These events are not brought on by a punishing hand in charge of the universe, but by our own actions and ignorance. And, as always, there are opportunities for the soul to learn.

Easy accessibility of world travel, and particularly travel to Eastern countries, as well as the increasing numbers of people migrating to the Western world have changed the face and thought patterns of the planet. Human rights legislation ensures that most people are free to practise their religions openly, thus exposing people from Western cultures to such philosophies as Buddhism and Hinduism.

Meditation techniques have become a normal part of our busy, stress-filled lives; multi-million dollar corporations encourage staff to use meditation for stress management. This is yet another spiritual truth that was buried but has been rediscovered.

The testimony of millions of long-term participants cannot be placed under a microscope, but neither can it be denied.

Public exposure to psychic phenomena has increased dramatically in the past decade. Movies, television programs and talk shows are presenting the public with true stories of psychic experiences from credible people. The gifted mediums in America are a joy to watch as they give undeniable proof of their abilities and the evidence that we survive the transition called death. This type of exposure starts people thinking and asking questions, wanting to see and know more, so that they can judge for themselves.

Exposure to this spiritual knowledge – to an understanding that there are far more dimensions in the universe than any of us might have realised; that everything we do affects others; that each lifetime on earth is a precious gift and opportunity; that life continues on beyond this earthly existence; that we live in a loving and supportive universe – all this and more leads each of us forward in terms of our own spiritual growth, and furthers the spiritual evolution of humankind.

$\mathscr{C}$LOSING THOUGHTS

I am demonstrating a very small part of the tremendous whole.
  Just as the earth cannot survive without life-giving water,
  psychic gifts cannot survive without spirituality.
  I am not a fortune teller and refuse to be linked with such.
  I rely entirely on spiritual communication directed by
  God's love to enlighten you and me.
  I give to you, in love, what God has given me to share with
humanity.
  My gifts cannot be bought or sold, nor can any price be fixed
on them.
  The fee is for my time.
  God bless
  Chang Tao

৵৵

I believe that all universal laws are important and that learning
to know and understand them is imperative. I have only written
here about the ones I deal with daily in my role as a medium.
Think about the consequences of the spiritual law regarding the
brotherhood of humankind. If we truly believe and feel that all
peoples are related to each other as a family, we become aware
that every person is ours to love, nurture and care for.

We are here on earth to grow as souls. Earth has no schools,

colleges or universities with the knowledge, structure or power
to lead and teach souls to reach enlightenment. But there are
places where people can learn about universal laws and how to
develop their healing, psychic and mediumistic abilities, and so
gain a better understanding of their soul's journey through this
life.

For most of us, though, our school is everyday life and the
experience we acquire as we make our earthly journey through
life after life, learning and growing from our mistakes. We die
many deaths, but it is only through the process of dying and
being born, time and time again, that we progress as souls.

In order to advance on our journey, we must not only learn
our own lessons; we must also help others to reach an understanding of what we have been able to learn. The universe is
our university, and those souls who are enlightened and reside
in the spirit realms are our teachers. They guide us along the
path and are our constant companions. The soul that believes it
has all the answers has not yet entered primary school.

When we work with psychic phenomena, we see spiritual laws
and principles in action. We learn to appreciate the Creator's
perfect plan for every soul. Our lives are perfect patterns. Remember, water is the most non-resistant element. If we want life to be
less of a struggle, we must be like water in the river; we must let
go and go with the flow, let the current gently take us with it,
knowing that we will be brought safely to the right destination
for us.

There are spiritual laws with which we live every day. How
we deal with them is our choice. All our words, deeds and
actions, good and bad, return to us. If we are unhappy, if we
feel trapped, we find ourselves inside a prison created by our
own fears. This is hell on earth. When we turn on the light of
knowledge, we will find there is nothing to fear from the God
of love, our Creator. Spiritual laws teach us about a loving
Creator, who has provided us with a beautiful planet on which
to experience earthly life with all its joys, triumphs and sorrows.

We are born with the memory of our true nature. All the
people living on earth know at some level that they have lived

before; they know how to heal themselves; they know they are immortal. The problem is that when we are born into this world, we are a long distance from our true homes, a long way from the source of our enlightenment. Still, we carry God's spark within us – it is the motor that drives the vehicle. The motor is the soul. The physical body is the vehicle we need for our existence in this world. Like all vehicles, it grows old and we die. But the divine spark within us – the soul – lives on.

Being here on earth is a great privilege and opportunity for each one of us, no matter how hard it might feel at the time. Being born is hard work. It isn't an experience that we welcome in the spirit world. It is impossible, however, not to learn from our earthly experiences. To come here and not take the full opportunity to learn as much as possible is a waste, but there are always new opportunities to learn and to grow.

The spiritual us is born of the light. Our natural abode is the light. When we set off on our journey towards birth, we are travelling away from the light and from our natural home. There is an instinctive part of each of us that will always make its way back there. In order to go back to the source of the light, we choose to go through birth and the earth life, as that is the only way to get closer to the light. Being born is far harder on the soul than dying is.

While it might be hard to grasp at first, the fact that we are of the light is as basic as water or air. And no matter how lost or misguided we become, however far we travel from the light, we are never totally lost. No matter what mistakes we've made, there is always the opportunity to start again.

Even though each of us will step through the doorway we call death, we will not cease to exist, nor does anyone else. Life goes on. Always there are the adventures of each lifetime and of life back in spirit between earthly lifetimes. Always there is the learning, the possibility for growth, and there are endless opportunities for us to practise daily acts of kindness.

❧

I believe everyone is capable of doing what I do. If you are developing your psychic awareness, do not limit yourself to any one area; explore, and expand your knowledge. Too often people get hung up on the tarot, crystals, numerology and the like. After a while, they won't do anything without consulting these props. What they should be doing is realising that there is much more to be discovered – and going out to search for it.

At the point of conception, the body is made up of the components of both the father and the mother, regardless of whether either individual is there once the child has come into the world. Even though we might never meet our birth father or mother in this lifetime, we did in fact choose them to be our parents. And even if we never know who our birth parents are in this life, we will know this when we return home to spirit.

∽∾

We are not alone in our life experience. We are all playing with very old scripts. There is not a thought, feeling or action that countless others have not experienced at other times and in other places. Moreover, we can learn from each other, as we see tremendous courage and self-sacrifice in others in times of extreme danger or difficulty. We are each other's teachers. And, although we might never, ever realise it, we may have deeply affected someone else's life with some kindness or some small act of courage when times were tough.

Whether or not we realise it, we live in a supportive, loving universe. This all-embracing love, that has as its purpose our growth towards the light, never fades. And just as this wonderful, divine love is constant, so, too, is the love we have for each other. Time, circumstance, even death cannot diminish this love. It, too, will never die.